YoungWriters
2004 POETRY COMPETITION

ONCE UPON A RHYME

IMAGINATION FOR
A NEW GENERATION

Northern Scotland

Edited by Donna Samworth

Nanny

D1102553

 Young**Writers**

First published in Great Britain in 2004 by:
Young Writers
Remus House
Coltsfoot Drive
Peterborough
PE2 9JX
Telephone: 01733 890066
Website: www.youngwriters.co.uk

SB ISBN 1 84460 491 8

Foreword

Young Writers was established in 1991 and has been passionately devoted to the promotion of reading and writing in children and young adults ever since. The quest continues today. Young Writers remains as committed to engendering the fostering of burgeoning poetic and literary talent as ever.

This year's Young Writers competition has proven as vibrant and dynamic as ever and we are delighted to present a showcase of the best poetry from across the UK. Each poem has been carefully selected from a wealth of *Once Upon A Rhyme* entries before ultimately being published in this, our twelfth primary school poetry series.

Once again, we have been supremely impressed by the overall high quality of the entries we have received. The imagination, energy and creativity which has gone into each young writer's entry made choosing the best poems a challenging and often difficult but ultimately hugely rewarding task - the general high standard of the work submitted amply vindicating this opportunity to bring their poetry to a larger appreciative audience.

We sincerely hope you are pleased with our final selection and that you will enjoy *Once Upon A Rhyme Northern Scotland* for many years to come.

Contents

Collace Primary School, Perth

Comrie Primary School, Copmrie

Luke Goddard (10)	38
Lucy Macdonald (10)	38
Rosie Turner (10)	39
Danielle-Louise Reid (10)	39
Erin Turner (10)	40
Laura Caldwell (10)	40
Christine Campbell (10)	41
Mariann Walker (10)	41
Zara Stewart (10)	42
Struan Carson (10)	43
Hayleigh Connor (10)	43
Henry Hunt (10)	44
Carrie Davidson (10)	44
Stephanie Kay (10)	45
Jamie Roxburgh (10)	45
Catherine Payne (10)	46
Natalie Moffat (10)	46

Conon Bridge Primary School, Dingwall

John Clark (7)	46
Jared De Kruijff (8)	47
Sarah Macdonald (7)	47
Shaun Reid	47
Ian Ross (7)	48
Andrew Kyle (7)	48
Lewis Mulhearn (8)	48
Logan Sinclair (7)	49
Alasdair Williamson (7)	49
Courtney Mackenzie (8)	49
Calum Cumming (7)	50
Callum Russell (7)	50
Neil Cameron (7)	50
Emily Fouka (8)	51
Innes Bushell (8)	51

Drakies Primary School, Inverness

Amy Piggot (11)	51
Chris Deacon (10)	52
Adam Kelly (10)	53
Stacey MacDonald (10)	54
Robbie Lorimer (10)	54

Sarah Harper (9)	55
Emma MacAulay (10)	55
Lesley Barron (10)	56
Craig Brand (10)	56
Gemma Ross (10)	57
Steven Fraser (10)	57
Alanna Goddard (10)	58
Robyn Stark (10)	58
Leigh-Anne Anderson (10)	59
Steven Ednie (10)	59
Kerry MacDonald (10)	60
Rachel MacDougall (10)	60
Brian Phillips (10)	61
Lucy Templeton (11)	61
Marc McPherson (10)	62
Jordan Cooper (10)	62
Chloe Reid (10)	62

Dunecht School, Westhill

Monique Hendy (8)	63
Mhairi Cargill (7)	63
Finlay McPherson (7)	64
Molly Spooner (8)	64
Cameron Brownie (7)	64
Kyla Hislop (8)	65
Hayley O'Brien (8)	65
Daniel Wilson (7)	65
Stephen Will (7)	66
Kerryn McRae (8)	66
Calum Rae (9)	66
Kenneth MacBeath (8)	67
Joanna Cook (8)	67
Sam Povey (8)	67
Michael Huntington (11)	68
Rachael Will (11)	69
Hannah Johnston (8)	69
James Huntington (9)	70
Christopher Huntington (9)	70
Shona MacBeath (11)	71
Aaron Brown (9)	71
Shona Thompson (11)	72

Kieran Brown (10)	72
Caitlin Drummond (9)	73
Stephanie Jane Malcolm (11)	73
Angus Wood (11)	74
Cameron Spooner (10)	75
Rhea Shearer (9)	76
Simon O'Brien (11)	77
Naomi Pearson (11)	78
Donna McGinley (10)	79
Rachel May Johnston (11)	79

East End Primary School, Elgin

Natasha Anderson (11)	80
Raye Hannah	80
Lauren Ford (11)	81
Matthew Tulip (11)	81
Sarah Mills (11)	82
Ross McGillivaray (11)	82
Samantha Tonberg (11)	83
Robert Mouncher (11)	83
Calum Leiper (11)	84
Staci Smith (12)	84
Darren Mair (10)	85
Kristoffer McKenzie (11)	85
Allan Watt (10)	86
Francesca Boyes (11)	86
Cameron Porter (10)	87
Fiona Meinen (11)	87
Katrina McIntosh (10)	88
Chloe O'Hare (12)	88
Emma McLennan (10)	89
Blossom McAfee (10)	89
Leanne Tonge (10)	90
Daniel Harrison (10)	91
Mark Stitt (11)	92
Sarah Anderson (10)	92
Steven Webster (11)	93
Hannah Scott (11)	94
Craig Ferguson (10)	95
Claire Grant (11)	96
Allan Slapp (11)	97

Grantown Primary School, Grantown-On-Spey

Samantha Watson (9)	97
Maisie Crake (9)	98
Kodie White (8)	98
Ryan Grant (9)	99
James Coutts (9)	99
Lauren Garside (9)	100
Hayley McFarlane (9)	100
James Towers (9)	100
Sarah Grant (9)	101
Joe Hopkins (9)	101
Megan Grant (9)	101
Alexandrea Macleod (9)	102
Ruairidh Murray (9)	102
Rosie Lean (9)	103
Adam Young (9)	103
Jessie Jones (9)	104
Greg Lawrence (9)	104
Iain Mackellar (9)	104
Adam Finlayson (9)	105
Rebecca Amphlett (9)	105
Markus Ruettimann (9)	105
Gregor Samuels (9)	106
Dean Morrison (9)	106
Gemma Beckwith (9)	106
Abigail Lavers (9)	107
Dayna McWhirter (9)	107
Alex Donaldson (9)	107
Jamie McWilliam (9)	108
Douglas Hay (9)	108

Greenloaning Primary School, Dunblane

Douglas Peter (8)	109
Jordan Reilly (9)	109
Gary McGlashan (10)	110
Amy McGlashan (7)	110
Lloyd Rumsby (7)	111
Maria Watson (9)	111

Hill Primary School, Blairgowrie

Paula Reid (11)	112
Ross Donald (11)	112
Jacquelyne MacDonald (11)	113
Lynn Harper (11)	113
Robyn Taylor (11)	114
Emma Oudney (11)	114
Laura Gibas (11)	115
Caitlin Duffy (11)	115
Alicia Beveridge (11)	116
Kevin Robb (11)	116
Rachael Lipp (11)	117
Holly Seager (11)	117
Fiona Ritchie (11)	118
Harley McIntyre (11)	118
Luke Grant (11)	119
John Ellis (11)	119
Zoe McLaren (11)	120
Daniel Anderson (11)	120
Lee Irvine (11)	121
John Cockburn (11)	121
Shauni Robinson (10)	122
Kris Nesbitt (11)	122
Ryan Lynn (11)	123
Ryan Feaks (11)	123
Robyn Smith (11)	124
Emily Cuthill (11)	125
Kathryn Forsyth (11)	126
Roy Edgar (11)	126
Hayley Douglas (11)	127
Grant Kellie (11)	127
Beth McIntyre (11)	128
Lori Cabena (11)	128
Finlay Page (11)	129
Rosie Wilson (11)	129
Calley Leith (11)	130
Hayley Grant (11)	131
Jamie Stewart (11)	132
Jade Webster (11)	132
Storm Andrews (11)	133
Matthew Parker (11)	133

Zoe Irvine (12) 134
Georgia Bell (11) 135

Invergarry Primary School, Invergarry
John Thomson (11) 135
Kelly MacDiarmid (10) 136
Laura Stewart (10) 136
Kirsty Mackenzie (9) 136
Alysha Henderson (9) 137
Rebecca Martin (10) 137
Robert Shepherd (10) 137
Matthew MacCallum (9) 138

Kilry Primary School, Blairgowrie
Daniel Channon (11) 138
Grant Walker (12) 138
Cameron Martindale (10) 139
Steven Walker (10) 139
Catriona Ferguson (9) 139
Gabriella Hall (11) 140
Rosalyn Hall (10) 140
Marcus De Vale (9) 141
Emma Bryce (9) 141

Marybank Primary School, Urray
Ross MacLeod (10) 142
Ryan MacMillan (10) 142
Fiona Fraser (11) 143
Blabheinn Mackintosh (10) 143
Helen Matheson (10) 143
Brian Finlayson (11) 144

Moncreiffe Primary School, Perth
James Smith (9) 144
Kirsteen MacSween (9) 145
Laura McLean (9) 145
Sam Edward (9) 146
Jodie McBeath (9) 146
Deanna Green (9) 147
Dean MacFarlane (9) 147

Molly Gibson (8)   163
Jacqueline Kindness (8)   163
Ryan Norrie (8)   163
Laura Simpson (9)   164
Amy Brain (8)   164

Scourie Primary School, Scourie by Lairg

Lucy Deakin (10)   165
Jo Fraser (10)   165
Sophie Deakin (8)   166
Eilidh MacFarlane (10)   166
Mathew Hathaway (8)   167

South Park School, Fraserburgh

Katie A Barnett (9)   167
Kirsten J Taylor (9)   168
Stephen Lippe (9)   168
Andrew Pirie (9)   168
Laura Hepburn (9)   169
Craig Barbour (9)   169
David Clark (9)   169
Emma McRae (9)   170
Marc Noble (9)   170
Lauren Buchan (9)   170
Andrew Reid (9)   171
Erin Beaton (9)   171

Stuartfield Primary School, Peterhead

Darren Milne (11)   172
Luke Duncan (11)   173
Stefanie Rhind (11)   173
Rachel McGinley (11)   174
Emma-Lee Davidson (11)   174
Beth Ann Gordon (11)   175
Jack Stott (11)   175
Jenna Elaine Thomson (11)   176
Danielle Jade Harper (10)   177
Nicola Ann Munro (11)   178
Kieran Connolly (11)   179
Kobi Poole (11)   180
Tanya Rose Rennie (11)   181

Westhill Primary School, Westhill

Christopher Ian Kelman (10)	182
Lauren Gale (12)	182
Kern Lasoki (11)	183
Jack Molyneux (12)	183
Cory Ogden (11)	184
Alyssa Warren (11)	184
Kieran Walden (11)	185
Calum Walker (11)	185
Craig Cuthbertson (11)	186
Lauren Swinhoe (11)	186
Ross Taylor (11)	187
Andrew James Skinner (11)	187
Kerry Milne (11)	188
Fiona Dixon (11)	188
Stephanie McMillan (11)	189
Jacqueline Wilson (11)	189
Calum Watson (11)	190
Naomi Howitt (11)	190
Fraser W McKain (12)	191
David Alexander Wright (11)	191
Natalie Watt (12)	192
Mark Drummond (11)	192
Peter Ronald (11)	193
Ruaridh Gollifer (11)	193

The Poems

The City

The city houses an army of ants
Rushing, always rushing.
Following the rules
Walk! Don't walk!
Red lights, green lights,
Never disobey
Standing in a queue,
Getting on a bus,
Ready to set of for work,
Following the giant crowd
Traffic jams galore
Rush hour has come again.

Hayley McKenzie (10)
Alehousewells Primary School, Kemnay

The Mountain

The mountain is a bear
Appealing but risky
She could steal your life in seconds.
A mountain can be calm in the winter,
A peaceful bear in hibernation.
But wake her . . .
And you are in trouble.
Her anger knows no bounds.
Spring comes
She awakens, surrounded by new life.
The mountain, mother of all creatures
That live upon her.

Stuart Reid (10)
Alehousewells Primary School, Kemnay

The Demolition Site!

A demolition site is like a T-rex
The ball and chain is like the tail of the dinosaur,
Smashing, crashing into walls
Ripping, tearing, crushing stuff till they crumple up
Chainsaws like teeth tearing into houses mincing them into rubble
Soon going out of control, destroying anything in its path
Shoving bricks and crushing them like they're body parts
Crushing, killing out of control soon everything falls.

Chay Milne (10)
Alehousewells Primary School, Kemnay

Health Food/Junk Food

Some foods are healthy,
Some foods are bad.
Some foods are sweet and tasty,
The best you've ever had.

Some people prefer chocolate,
Cola, candy canes.
But some people eat healthy stuff,
To stop the stomach pains.

Some people drink milk,
To help their teeth go white.
Some people drink cola,
Well into the night.

I do like sweets,
Once in a while,
But only a little,
Not a big pile.

But when I turn and take a glance,
At people giving a diet a chance,
They only go for a week or so,
Because they can't let the sweet stuff go!

Jordan Orr (9)
Alvie Primary School, Kincraig

Rumplestiltskin

The slave went out and he was to blame,
He told everyone about his daughter,
Which was a shame.
The king went to him and said,
'Come here old man and look at this thread.'
The slave said to the king,
'My daughter can do this, apart from one thing!'
Still, she went not knowing anything!
She walked along and started to sing.
She went to the king and he locked her up,
She sat beside the rotted cup.
With all the shining gold lying there,
She did not know what to bare.
Suddenly a puff of smoke appeared with a little man about to choke.
He said to her,
'I'll spin this thread, if you give me something instead.'
She gave him her jewels until they were gone,
He said to her,
'Tell me my name and I'll leave you alone.'
She took a deep breath and counted to three,
Rumplestiltskin is your name.

Christie McInnes (11)
Alvie Primary School, Kincraig

Snake

S lithering along the ground
N astiest reptile to be found
A mazing appetite!
K iller bite!
E ats too much food, a long sleep would be good.

Karys Crook (9)
Alvie Primary School, Kincraig

School Trip

'Right class sit down.
I am going to tell you where we are going on our school trip.
No Marsha we are not going to France.
What is it Victoria?
No you can't bring your horse.
Marsha I have told you we are not going to France.
Yes Leanne?
No Leanne, you can't bring your football.
Right what I was going to tell you?
What is it Leanne?
No you can't bring your dog.
But Victoria is not bringing her horse.
Right we are going.
But where are we going?
I did not have time to tell you
We are late!'

Fiona Dudgeon (10)
Alvie Primary School, Kincraig

The Deserted House

No carpets on the floor.
No handle on the door.
No curtains to pull tight.
No furniture clean and bright.

The floorboards creaked.
The shabby roof leaked.
The spiders' webs grew.
Through broken windows, birds flew.

All around the house was sad.
Nothing there to make you feel glad.
Alone and lonely it would stay.
A deserted house till its dying day.

Morgan Evans (11)
Alvie Primary School, Kincraig

Snakes

A stupid little fisherman
Avoids the laws of nature.
To fish along the little pier,
Is his only objective.

He sits on the pier,
As the sun is getting hotter.
He doesn't pay attention,
To the ripple in the water.

A snake of tremendous size,
Shoots at him like greased lightning.
It swallows him whole,
Before he can start fighting.

The police they arrive,
Take a gun and blow it apart.
They save the fisherman,
That's a good start.

His body was crippled,
His bones were all smashed.
He was all bloody,
His organs had crashed.

If you don't know
What's in your wake,
Don't fish off a pier,
Where there might be a *snake!*

Seòras Orr (11)
Alvie Primary School, Kincraig

My Pet Snake

I had a snake,
His name was Jake,
He had the friendliest smile.
But when Jake tried to kiss my friends,
They always ran a mile!

Aaron Paterson (11)
Alvie Primary School, Kincraig

The Battle Of The Year

The rain beat down on the ground,
The tiger prowled around,
The men held their spears, three feet in height,
The leader of the tribe shouted out, *'Fight!'*

The men ran screaming, knives drawn,
Could they hold off the beasts till dawn?
There was a howl, as a tiger impaled itself on a spear,
This was definitely going to be, the battle of the year.

Seven men against thirty-odd beasts,
If the men pulled this off they'd have many feasts.
The rock it got sprayed with tigers' blood,
A man fell and got covered in mud.

But he was back up but a paw to the face,
Left him on the floor, his head up in space,
Twenty more beasts for the six men to kill,
The beasts were doing well, until . . .

A flash of lightning sparked the grass,
A burst of flame turned into a mass,
Of howling and yelping all over the hill,
Three men were killed, three left to kill.

But the tigers retreat because of the fire,
The flames slowly licked higher and higher.

The humans won the battle, the tigers were gone!
The rain died away and out the light shone!

Sean MacDonald (11)
Alvie Primary School, Kincraig

The Three Little Pigs

The three little pigs had to move home,
But the three little pigs did not much moan.
They went to a man who worked in a shop
And stupidly did not buy a padlock.

The first little pig bought some straw,
But had to go back and get some more.
The second little pig bought some sticks
And the third little pig bought some bricks.

The big bad wolf went for a wander one day,
He wanted to go in but had to pay.
But the big bad wolf had nothing to give
And as you know the wolf did not want him to live.

So he huffed and he puffed and blew the house down
And the little pig ran to the house of sticks with a frown.
The big bad wolf waited a while,
Then had an idea and started to smile.

He went to the house of sticks with his smile,
He huffed and he puffed but took a while.
Eventually he blew down the house of sticks,
But they were already at the house of bricks.

So he himself went to the house thinking he was a brave man,
But the three little pigs already had a plan.
They made fire in a pan
And put it under the chimney.

And can you guess what happens next?

Charley Newman (9)
Alvie Primary School, Kincraig

Changing Seasons

In the woods, trees swaying left to right,
Crashing together, having a fight.
The wind blows hard!
Leaves fall like a floating card.

Then the weather changes into sun!
Lots of people having fun.
The flowers pop out
As the sun gives a shout.

Now it's winter, snow all around.
Clean and bright on the ground.
Now the trees don't make a sound
And there's no wildlife to be found.

Now it's spring, we go out to play.
Life is back to normal until another day.

Scott Dixon (9)
Alvie Primary School, Kincraig

My Puppy

My puppy
Silky brown and white,
Playful, energetic, bouncy,
Like a baby kangaroo,
Like a baby kitten,
He makes me feel happy. I love him,
Like opening my presents,
My puppy,
Makes me long to stroke him.

Oliver Addyman (9)
Ardvreck School, Crieff

Staff Loos

I am silver and throw back all I see.
I am not cruel only truthful.
People come and go,
They examine me all the time.
Children reject me.
Only adults come into my range,
Some do their hair or their make-up,
But others just peep then go.

Cleaners polish me, then leave.
I am shiny now.
Then a light goes out,
I am left in darkness.
No one needs me anymore.
I am alone,
Waiting for tomorrow,
For someone to come.

Camilla Ambler (11)
Ardvreck School, Crieff

The Goldfish

A scaly swimmer
Fast, shiny and slippery
Like a giant shark
Like a slimy slug
Makes me want to catch him
Like a monkey in the cage
The goldfish
It reminds me of how big the sea is.

Sean Watson (9)
Ardvreck School, Crieff

The Royal Mirror

I am silver and precise
Faithful and faultless
Impregnable yet delicate
I am the all seeing eye
Regal but beautiful
My heart is of gold
I gaze upon the contrasting wall
So long I have done so
It is a part of my cold heart

And there a young woman stands
Marvelling at her beauty
She comes and goes like the wind
To me she is the true companion
She comes to me in a wave of robes
Her face is angelic yet anxious
She leaves and I am plunged into darkness

The room is awakened
And I carry on my gaze
Many people wade into me
Tears and despair fill the room
Like a terrible plague
Never to cease
Many a long year has gone by
Yet her face shall never die

And now everything has gone
I still carry my endless stare.

Gardie James Duff (10)
Ardvreck School, Crieff

Pub Mirror

I am old and wise.
I am familiar with these brutal times.
People gaze at me, their pupils grow in distress.
Smoke fills the room like a ghostly plague.
All I see are hazy figures.
A glass hits the floor shattering into thousands of stars.
Thumping of a fist on a table, followed by a shout.

It is quiet now.
The lights are out.
No sound of glass or shouting.
A crack floods with pain.
A brushing noise, as a broom sweeps past
Moving everything in its path.
Darkness comes over me.
I am ready for the next day.

Fergus Bevens (10)
Ardvreck School, Crieff

Mirror In A Classroom

I am simple and precise, I see all.
My heart is the opposite wall.
I am merciless without intent.
All I reflect is the truth.
I have no expectations.

Little faces walking into view every day,
I have smudges over my all seeing eye.
A teacher comes into view day after day
She is like a distressed animal,
A victim of the truth.

Campbell Findlay (11)
Ardvreck School, Crieff

Hairdresser's Mirror

I am honest and precise. I do not falsify.
I see people, I see pots.
I cannot wink, I cannot blink.
I gaze wondrously at the face ahead.
Different faces come and go,
In and out, back and forth.
I absorb them loyally.
Mixed senses, assorted styles.

People contemplate,
Some perturbed, others not.
When there are no people, no faces.
I stare at the conflicting wall.
Through the vast window,
I watch the sun go down,
I wish I was free.

Nancy Rowan-Hamilton (11)
Ardvreck School, Crieff

A Hairdresser's Mirror

I am important and definite
I never lie to those who gaze
Into my eyes.

It is morning, she comes, someone else behind her.
She sits before me, the other one remains standing
Then cuts, snips, transforms.
It seems like decades before she is finished.
The transformed woman looks into me,
Frowning, not happy with the truth.
They leave, darkness returns until morning,
Then they come once more.

Amelia Bayler (10)
Ardvreck School, Crieff

Tunisia

I went there some time ago
There I had fun
We went to night parties
And there we sang songs
After breakfast I ran outside
And dived in the pool.

My brother got a tattoo
But some bits came off
As he entered the pool
We went through the desert
On some camels
And got off to have some tea
We took our hats off
Back in the bus
And back to the hotel.

The next morning
We saw the sunset
But all I did was look at
The massive beetles.

Henry Rymer (10)
Ardvreck School, Crieff

Dorm Mirror

The morning brings light
And children are running and jumping
Getting changed four times a day
Most of the time I am lonely
Sometimes my face is cleaned
And I can see more clearly
My life is ever so boring
People leave me all alone
My life is ever so boring.

Annabel Blackett (10)
Ardvreck School, Crieff

Tractor Mirror

I am exact
My back is black
My face is silver
I reflect what I see.
With no delay
The moment it appears
Sometime moved from
My stiff position.

One minute I see the road
The next I see the grey dark sheds
What is this, an earthquake?
No, it is just the engine starting.
I am moving now, to a new place
Ready for new visions.

Jack Cadzow (10)
Ardvreck School, Crieff

The Rabbit

Lives in a warren
Huddles, jumps, leaps
Just like a cat, when it is playing
Just like a kangaroo hopping
Through the desert
It makes me feel relaxed
It feels like a bird in the sky
Rabbit
A soft, cuddly animal to be looked after.

Gemma Ives (8)
Ardvreck School, Crieff

Findlay Hall Mirror

I am silver and exact
I can only tell the truth
I look at the climbing wall
Nearly all of the time
I see the children come
The noises start
Some of them look at themselves
Goal!
The boy looks at himself
At the end of the game
The children go
The light turns out
For another night.

James Salisbury (10)
Ardvreck School, Crieff

I Wish I Was There

America
Shy crocodiles
Weedy swamp
And steamy pools
Rumbling motorbike
Sometimes windy
Sometimes still
But always hot
Night brings rain and thunder
I eventually sleep.

Stuart Gray (10)
Ardvreck School, Crieff

Wishing I Was In Dunk Island

Small gliding plane,
Riding over the dunes,
Glittering rows of sand,
Cities of coral under the sea,
Bees in their hive,
A jacuzzi that makes your spine tickle.

A burning sun,
Marble white hills,
Tropical rain
That beats down on the emerald leaves,
Ruby sunset on the shimmering shores,
Elephant-like hills
I want to go back.

William Reynolds (9)
Ardvreck School, Crieff

The Sun

Peacefully, the birds swoop and soar
Waves rolling over and over
I rise bringing children with me
Running on the everlasting sand dunes
I watch, wishing I too could be minute
Laughing and joking
But I know I am the light in the world
People come and go though there are still sunbathers lying too
A feisty breeze stirs
The blood-red poppies which mingle with the dull green grass
Stars appear, one, two, three . . . one million
I set and the birds swoop and soar once more.

Annabel Troughton (10)
Ardvreck School, Crieff

My Granny's House

I wish I was there,
Playing hide-and-seek,
Diving under beds.
Waiting in my secret world
To be found.

Baking a cake,
A chocolate sponge,
Smarties on top,
Waiting to be eaten,
To be enjoyed.

Feeding the ponies,
Talking away,
Preparing the food
Which is waiting to be swallowed
To be eaten.

Kitty Rowan Hamilton (9)
Ardvreck School, Crieff

Fernie BC

I will arise and go now to Fernie BC.
I will make the ice puddles.
I will feel the soft but cold snowflakes on my tongue.
I will crush the snow under my feet.
Always cold.
The frosty leaves will crackle as I walk by.
Snow falls off the mountain.
The icy winds brush through my hair.
As I sledge down the hill, looking at the soft snow ahead.
Then I will lie in my bed and watch the snow fall
Listening to the deadly silence.

Pippi Russell (9)
Ardvreck School, Crieff

I Remember Fyvie

I remember the snow in the winter at Fyvie
I hear the crunch of snow below my feet
I feel the icicles drip on my head
And soft snowflakes on my nose.

I remember the thrill
Of shooting down the hill
On a sledge, racing my brothers
The whip of wind on my face.

The whack of a snowball
Hitting my back
And hearing the laughter
Of my brother behind me.

When I reach the door
I smell my hot supper
Then I slip on the
ice
    covered
        gravel.

Josie Leader (9)
Ardvreck School, Crieff

The Badger

As strong as ten men
Black, white, fierce
As black as night
As white as clouds can get
It makes me feel strong
He fights for his family
The badger
It is sad that they are nearly extinct.

Andrew Orr Ewing (9)
Ardvreck School, Crieff

New York City

The horns beeping
As I listen through the window,
People walking down the street,
When I go downstairs
And go outside
I feel the heat
From the sun.

And dive in the pool
Which is so cool.
With butterflies fluttering
In the air.

But in the winter
Oh it's chilly and cold
So I would fly now
And fly to New York City.

Stephanie Burt (9)
Ardvreck School, Crieff

The Sycamore

I can feel cold grass between my toes
Time to wear short clothes
I can feel the breeze pleasant on my face
Then I lie at the base of a tree
Now I will listen to the bee

I see the leaves on the tree
As though they were waving at me.
I suck juice through a straw
My dog loose in the garden
Then I will watch the sun as it sinks behind the sky
It's here I love to lie.

Atlanta Pritchard Barrett (9)
Ardvreck School, Crieff

North Uist

I wish I was there, I wish I was there today,
I wish I was there from June to May,
I miss the salmon leap
And forever these memories I keep.

Somehow I know this is where I belong,
The words I speak are clearly not wrong,
I miss the brightness of home
And the waves splashing calmly to bubbling foam.

I miss the air-shocking fire of the gun,
And the slow, steady rise of the morning sun,
The swishing of the water in the bay,
I must go now without delay.

Hector Bulmer (10)
Ardvreck School, Crieff

Sunny Beaches

My mind is there,
On the golden sand
Feeling the water trickling
In-between my toes.

The odour of popcorn
Wafting through the air
Children demanding another ice cream!
Then building gigantic sandcastles
Watching the waves take them away.

Gazing for huge crabs
In the summery rock pools,
Then packing up the picnic
And leaving the wonderful beach.

Dougie Critchley (9)
Ardvreck School, Crieff

Wishing I Was There

I wish I was there
Climbing the rocks
Watch the fishing boats
Sail back to the docks.

I wish I was there
Dozing on the sand
Listening to the seagulls
With a sandwich in my hand.

Walks on the beach
Then the chip shop we'd reach
Oh the smell and the taste
Not one we would waste.

The paper concealed
But we'd rip and reveal
I wish I was there
Back in beautiful Ayr.

Sophie Thompson (10)
Ardvreck School, Crieff

Polzeath

The gulls calling,
The smell of chips from the bar.

The waves rolling in,
Eating away at the cliffs.

Sand everywhere,
All piled into castles.

Beaches so long you
Can't see the waves.

I wish I was there.

Max Rivers (10)
Ardvreck School, Crieff

A Periscope

I am precise and clear.
If I am not, I am replaced or disposed of.
I am used in conjunction with another mirror to present
                                    the outside world.
Protecting me, is a sheet of glass.
I never get cleaned.

Whilst propelling through the sea,
I observe extraordinary creatures surrounding me,
Suddenly I see a torpedo advancing for my bulk.
It hits me square.
I am dispersed,
Now I lay useless on the seabed.

Lewis Fyfe (11)
Ardvreck School, Crieff

Holy Island

On my back, on the sand,
In the middle of no man's land,
Getting up to go home,
Coming back with an awful moan,
I will return another day,
Somehow I will find a way to be on my own
Where no one knows,
The white sand trickling through my toes.

Jumping out of the boat at night,
Hauling back in, with all my might,
Then find in a grassy dune
And just waiting for the stars and the moon.

Rory Townsend-Rose (10)
Ardvreck School, Crieff

The Changing Room Mirror

I am lustrous and precise.
I draw no conclusions.
Whatever I see I devour politely.
I see curtains in front of me,
But have never seen past it.
People come,
They try on clothes,
They smile,
They curse.
They do not like the truth I show.
They stare into me with aggression,
But some like what they see.

Hattie Mellor (10)
Ardvreck School, Crieff

The Waterfall

I dive into the chilly water
Then tumble onto the shiny rocks
Water descending rapidly on me
Pine needles make cushions for my feet
Water buffeting below me
Bashing the bottom with all its might
Splattering the pool.
When I reach the summit
I think before, then go
Diving into the shadowy blue water
And then . . .
Gliding up to the surface
Back into my own world.

Charlotte Houldsworth (9)
Ardvreck School, Crieff

Shop Changing Room Mirror

I am faithful. I do not prevaricate.
I reveal only the truth.
Most of the time I gaze at the curtain opposite.
It is blue with red stripes. It seems to twinkle.
Other times I reflect moving figures.
They either idolise or despise.

I see darkness, then I see light.
People stand over me like they expect to see what they want.
I am blamed for what I tell,
Yet I am truthful, not ferocious.
I am important to them, they need me.
I soak up what I see, day after day, night after night.

Tara Gladstone (11)
Ardvreck School, Crieff

The English Rugby Team

They won the World Cup
They're strong, powerful, fearless
Like 15 fearless lions
Like a cat versus a mouse
It makes me feel powerful
Like a robust jaguar
The English rugby team
They are unbeatable.

John Empson (9)
Ardvreck School, Crieff

Novato

I will arise and go to Novato
For I need lots of warmth.
I would love to go to the sunshine again.
I will arise and go now and go to the land of Novato
Joy and happiness will come to me, for I am sick of the rain.
I will arise and go now,
For I am sick of the cold.
I will arise and go now,
For I need some peace in me.
I will arise and go now, and go to Novato,
I will arise and go, away from my country.

Lochlann Robertson   (10)
Ardvreck School, Crieff

St Andrew's Beach

I wish I was there,
On the sandy, shelly landscape,
I wish I could see the rocky pools,
With tiny fish and hiding crabs,
And the jellyfish waiting to be swept
Back into the sea.
I wish I could see the gushing waves
Licking the sandy beach,
The immense sand dunes
With crunchy seaweed on top,
And kites, flying in the sky.

Struan Robertson   (10)
Ardvreck School, Crieff

Rome

I wish I was there,
In the capital of the land of pasta and pizza,
Where in the summer the sun soars high
And the winter storms crash overhead in the sky,
There are many sights to see,
The Colosseum where so long ago,
Brave warriors would fight,
The Spanish steps,
I'm tired before the top,
The Trevi Fountain too,
Throw in a coin and I will go back some day,
To the shop with 100 ice cream flavours,
Where you're sure to find your taste,
Pistachio, lemon, strawberry, raspberry and more,
Paddling pools in every garden,
So cool in the summer,
The language of Italian too,
So beautiful in many ways,
Cats in the night,
Which yowl and fight,
But that's the only down,
Oh Roma, Rome, Rome,
I open my eyes
And see the blank page of my jotter,
Now I know what to write!
I wish I was there.

Corinna Harrison (9)
Ardvreck School, Crieff

Barbados

I wake up every morning and go for a swim,
I hear fountain splashes,
On the beach,
The sand cushions my feet
And the seagulls squawking above my head,
The sound of boat engines starting up,
Girls and boys shout and scream,
On the banana boat,
Waves splash over my head,
Getting tired now,
So get into bed,
The crickets sing and surround the house
In the dark sitting on the cold, hard concrete.

Iona McHardy (10)
Ardvreck School, Crieff

Skiing In America

I wish I was there
Building snowmen,
After a great day skiing.
Going over jumps,
Soothing hot chocolate,
Then back to skiing in powder up to my knees.
A great lunch
Then a warm shower.
Pizza for supper,
Next to the cosy fire
I wish I was there,
Having a snowball fight with my brother.

Jemima Reid (10)
Ardvreck School, Crieff

Wishing I Was There

The smell of fresh flowers,
The familiar flavour of home baking,
Melting in my mouth,
Playing with Madge,
Bolting through woods,
Dodging the trees,
Firing arrows high in the air.

Planting potatoes,
Going for a stroll,
Making catapults then firing them,
Collecting the wood; Madge in the way.

The taste of Sprite bubbling on my tongue,
Taking in the luxurious surrounds,
The only time I feel excited,
The best 24 hours of my life.

Hamish Tester (10)
Ardvreck School, Crieff

The Hedgehog

The hedgehog
It wears a spiky coat
Slow, prickly and cute
It's like a little ball of needles
Like a turtle with spikes
It makes me feel huge
Like an enormous giant that everyone notices
The hedgehog
Reminds us that we're not that prickly!

Alice Hay (9)
Ardvreck School, Crieff

Islay

I love to go back to Islay
To hear the waves washing the shore
To run on the sandy beach
Slide down the silken dunes
Hear the early morning
Owls hooting
Then in the day I would go golfing
And sailing along the flowing sea
I hear the pond water rippling
And the blow hole forcing water skywards
I love to go fishing there
And crabbing in the busy rock pools
My heart will stay there forever.

Rory Maclachlan (10)
Ardvreck School, Crieff

My Dog

My dog
Always looking for food
Black, sleepy, fast
Like a champion swimmer
Like a running cheetah
It makes me feel proud to be his owner
Like the king of beasts
My dog
Reminds my family how lucky we are.

Archie Troughton (8)
Ardvreck School, Crieff

Loch Hourn

My heart is in the country,
My heart is not here.
It's with the buzzing of bees
And the fresh morning pine,
It's with the splashing of waves
And the water's ripple.

My heart is in the country,
My heart is not here.
It's with the cold, icy sea
And the tugging of desperate fish on my line,
My heart is in the country,
My heart is not here.

Patrick Russell (10)
Ardvreck School, Crieff

The Water Slide

Stairs are going up,
Getting steeper and steeper as we go,
Waiting in the cramped up queue,
Looking around the corners,
To see people go whooshing down,
Now it's my turn,
I swish and slide round corners,
Hear people shouting and screaming
Splash!
I am down
I think I'll go again.

Alice Onslow (9)
Ardvreck School, Crieff

Undersea Poem

In the deep blue sea there are
Ten octopuses swimming and squelching
Nine clownfish wiggling their tails
Eight sharks chomping lots of fish
Seven shrimps crawling along
Six eels swimming and moving from side to side
Five pufferfish puffing out their tummies
Four whales big and strong
Three jellyfish boinging up and down
Two sea horses going neigh!
One, gulp! Guess what?

Thomas Crosthwaite (9)
Ardvreck School, Crieff

A Day in Campbeltown

I get up in the moonlit morning,
And think of all the things I hope to do,
I will walk along the pebbly beaches,
Hearing shells crunch beneath my feet,
And feel waves crash against my legs.

I will wade in the choppy sea,
Build a sandcastle or two,
As the gulls caw and swoop,
And forage for their evening meal,
Then I will count the gulls as I go to sleep.

James Gray (10)
Ardvreck School, Crieff

When I Go Under The Sea

When I go under the sea,
I see fishes racing by me.

When I go under the sea,
I see dolphins jumping by me.

When I go under the sea,
I see sharks snapping by me.

When I go under the sea,
I see crabs crawling by me.

When I go under the sea,
I see jellyfish wobbling by me.

When I go under the sea,
I see bubbles rising above me.

Andrina Dew (9)
Ardvreck School, Crieff

Cats

Cats,
Come in all sorts of colours,
Sleek, smooth, silky,
Like a hunter with a gun,
Like a lion stalking prey,
I long to stroke him,
Like a tiny kitten,
Cats,
Queen of the animals.

Duncan McFarlane (9)
Ardvreck School, Crieff

Thomas' Pets

In his bedroom, Thomas kept
Ten dogs that slept under the bed
Nine snakes that squirmed around
Eight monkeys that were always eating bananas
Seven spiders making webs
Six alligators snapping at the monkeys
Five snails eating leaves
Four lizards going berserk
Three dinosaurs crushing the house
Two elephants squirting water
And *one* . . . guess what?

Thomas Riddell-Webster (8)
Ardvreck School, Crieff

Sottish Rugby Team

Scottish rugby team
A strong, united team
Fast, fierce, fearless
Like a tiger against a kitten
Like a champion runner
It makes me feel proud
Like getting an A
Scottish rugby team
Reminds Scotland how lucky we are.

Simon Carmichael (9)
Ardvreck School, Crieff

Addis Ababa

My heart is in Ethiopia
Where the blazing sun shines
And the animals graze
On the spiky, dead pasture.

My heart is in Ethiopia
Where hyenas crawl out
In the dead of night
And fight to the death.

My heart is in Ethiopia
Where the long grass was
As yellow as a banana skin
And I hid in it.

Francis Sherlock (10)
Ardvreck School, Crieff

Going To The White Cottage

I will arise and go now
To the warm feeling of the white cottage
And I'll stay for a week.
The dogs will chase the sheep
As I lie in bed with the wind
Roaring and the water pouring
Onto the white cliffs
As the owls call.

Henry Ambler (9)
Ardvreck School, Crieff

Betty Blue

The fluffy blue
Of the house - Betty Blue

The pussy
With the softest blue fur - Betty Blue

The cat that pads through the house
Soundless

The one whose fur
Is like sky,
Like a blue cloud
Looking around the house

Betty Blue, how gracefully
She spreads her claws
And pads around the mattress
Making herself a bed

Where she'll dream
She could be a bird!
Soaring through the sky
Feeling the wind through her fur

And soar for miles on end,
To her paradise, on a sunny island
Where all her troubles would go away
And she'd purr.

Catriona Ianneta-Mackay (9)
Collace Primary School, Perth

The Writer Of This Poem

(Based on 'The Writer Of This Poem' b y Roger MdGough)

The writer of this poem . . .
Is as tall as a tree,
As keen as mustard
And as sporty as can be.

As strong as an axe
As fast as a dog,
He quite likes farming
But acts like a hog.

As hard as rock
As cold as snow,
As sharp as a knife,
As cool as man can know.

The writer of this poem . . .
Always gets in a pickle
He usually annoys his friends
(By giving them a tickle!)

Ewan Penny (9)
Collace Primary School, Perth

The Shark

A true water king
If ever something could swim
He'd beat them in a flash.

Rows of teeth
For slashing meat
A hunger of the deep.

An express train of the waterways
Until something comes along
Evil with two arms and legs
Will hunt him till he's gone.

Stefan Brzeski (10)
Comrie Primary School, Comrie

Autumn

The delicate purple thistle,
Dancing in the autumn breeze.
The helicopter seed pods,
Falling from the trees.

The sentimental oak tree,
Standing lonely in the woods.
The tantalising rainbow,
Taking all of nature's goods.

Now those days are over,
The landscape's been destroyed.
Pollution, fumes and gasses,
Create a toxic void.

Chloe Finlayson (10)
Comrie Primary School, Comrie

The Golden Eagle

See the golden eagle as it swooped down on its prey
Then a wee squeal as it moves away.
Its talons of steel, see how they grab its meal
By the end of the day see how it finishes off its prey.

Peter Muirhead (10)
Comrie Primary School, Comrie

The Great Eagle

The legendary great eagle with claw-like talons
and a beak as sharp as knives.
It flies so gracefully and will eat anything in sight
until the eggs hatch.
One left in a poacher's cage and the eagle was set free.

Aidan Copeland (10)
Comrie Primary School, Comrie

The White Lion Legend

The last white lion
Stalking through the plains
Big fangs, sharp claws,
Impressive white mane.
Legend says when the last one walks
The world is meant to end.
Now its cubs have all been taken
By mean and greedy men.

He's hungry and he's thirsty
With sorrow in his heart.
He is meant to be a guardian,
The keeper of the world.
When he is gone the sun will fade
The light will never shine.
Help keep him here or life will end.
His life is also mine.

Luke Goddard (10)
Comrie Primary School, Comrie

Vicky

Vicky she had grace.
But now I can't touch her delicate face.
Every time we would laugh and play,
She would stay with me all day.
When she would have a rest
I would try and be the best.

Oh Vicky you belong to the heavens,
It is a better world,
But how I wish I could see you once more before my life had whirled.
I still cry for you because you were special and still are.
I'll never forget you from afar.

Lucy Macdonald (10)
Comrie Primary School, Comrie

The Long Thing

There once was a long thing
It reached up to the sky
The owner of the long thing
Was very big and shy.

He was yellow and brown all over
His eyes and ears were brown
When he falls asleep
He always crouches down.

The tall, thin animal
Was always a laugh
No wonder he has a long neck
After all he is a giraffe.

Rosie Turner (10)
Comrie Primary School, Comrie

Never Leave

Never leave, oh never leave
Don't leave me here alone.
You know what I'd be like
I'd never leave home.

Never go, oh never go
Don't leave me here
On my own.

I won't survive
I won't feel alive
Never go, please no.

You are my life you are my soul.
Don't leave, don't go.

Danielle-Louise Reid (10)
Comrie Primary School, Comrie

I Love My Bunny

I love my bunny,
He is fat and black,
With big, long ears
And a little fluffy tail.

He sees with his big brown eyes,
And licks with his long, rough tongue,
He has big, black ears
And long, white whiskers,
He has a very fluffy head.

My bunny eats two handfuls of food a day,
And likes to chomp on grass,
He also likes fresh new hay
And a little bowl of water.

I love my bunny,
He loves me too,
I'm sure,
I think,
I know.

Erin Turner (10)
Comrie Primary School, Comrie

The Slinky Silky Sly Cat

The slinky, silky, sly cat
Peeked round the door
The slinky, silky, sly cat
Crouched down on the floor

Her eyes are sharp
Her ears are pricked
She sneaks around
She's willing for a fight

Then suddenly, she pounces
And the mouse is out of sight.

Laura Caldwell (10)
Comrie Primary School, Comrie

The Biggest Bird Of Prey

The biggest bird of prey,
As I watched it glide and sway,
Its golden eyes shone brightly in the sky,
Searching for its prey.

Its mighty wings,
Reached the sky,
Pumped the air
And rose up high.

It looked around from its miraculous height
And then a rabbit came in its sight,
The chase was on,
It would go on all night,
The eagle would win with power and might.

As it bit its tasty meal,
The poor little rabbit gave a fatal squeal.
It was dead its life had come to an end,
Away the eagle flew its eaglets to tend.

Christine Campbell (10)
Comrie Primary School, Comrie

The Penguin

My colours are a mix of dark and light
I have to brag that it's such a beautiful sight.
My father took care of me when I was just an egg
I catch my food I don't have to beg.
I swim in a cold river
I like it, I don't shake or shiver
I waddle round, I like to play
Even in blizzards it's a beautiful day
Do you know me I'll be at the zoo
Or if you go to the South Pole
You'll see me there too.

Mariann Walker (10)
Comrie Primary School, Comrie

The Months Of The Year

January brings the snow
Makes toes and fingers glow

February brings the rain
That thaws the frozen ponds again

March brings breezes loud and shrill
Stirs the dancing daffodil

April bring flocks of pretty lambs
Jumping round their fleecy dams

May brings primrose sweet
Laying flowers at our feet

June brings tulips, lilies, roses
Fills the children's hands with posies

Hot July brings cooling showers
Strawberries and pretty flowers

August brings the breeze again
The sailing boats come and go again

September brings sheaves of corn
Then the harvest home is born

Fresh October brings the leaves that fall
Ivy dying on the garden wall

Dull November brings the blast
Rain is falling very fast

December brings the sleet
Children waiting for their Christmas treat.

Zara Stewart (10)
Comrie Primary School, Comrie

Monkey Time

It swings through the air like it doesn't care,
His friends come and fall down the stairs,
One of them starts to mime,
Yeah, it's monkey time!

All the monkeys play,
And they all say,
They're having a great time,
Yeah, I'm better than fine!

Monkey time birds fly away,
The music is loud while they play,
They couldn't believe their eyes,
The orang-utan has arrived.

Suddenly it stops,
It goes away and squats,
It's away to mime,
Bye-bye, monkey time!

Struan Carson (10)
Comrie Primary School, Comrie

Moving On

It's hard to leave good friends behind
To move on not knowing what I'll find
Unknown lands far ahead
And known one's far behind.

Going somewhere I've never been before
Living near new friends
Opening brand new doors.

I keep on walking around the world
Never stopping still
Till I find the place where I should be
Then stop and make a den till I move on again.

Hayleigh Connor (10)
Comrie Primary School, Comrie

Zombie Walk

The zombie will follow you wherever you go
Through storms through hurricanes and snow
A tiger or bear won't help you
You will have a better chance with a yo-yo

Help me! Help me! You'll say
But it's hopeless just hopeless the help won't come for another day
You'll run, you'll run
But he will still come

Suddenly it's silent you're in a shed
Then out of the blue
He jumps on you
And you're dead! Dead! Dead!

Just remember he'll be after you.

Henry Hunt (10)
Comrie Primary School, Comrie

Newborn Kitten

I'm warm inside
My whiskers flopping side to side
My paws sore and annoying my mind
Even still I'm sleepy inside

My mum's sitting beside me,
That means no one will touch me
She's purring in my ears
Then I finish all my tea.

Later on through the night
I know to go outside
For my night-time break
I know I have a warm
Bed waiting inside.

Carrie Davidson (10)
Comrie Primary School, Comrie

My Lovely Cat

I love my cat she's big and fat
And black all over.
She likes to cause trouble and tries to be tough
With her big, white, sharp paws.

She gets her big, fat tongue and licks me all the time
And when you stand on her foot,
She cries until water comes out of her eyes
And goes down her black chest.

I just love my cat with black all over,
I would not change anything.
Put my lovely, big brown eyed cat away to someone else
Why should I?
She is a good cat and she's got a lovely smile.

Stephanie Kay (10)
Comrie Primary School, Comrie

The Otter

As the otter comes out of the water
His dark green eyes reflect off the sun.
His soft padded paws, nice and smooth
See how he hunts, in and out of the water,
With a fish hanging out of his mouth.

He curls up and slowly drifts into a deep sleep,
With exciting thoughts running through his head
About how he had filled himself with nice, juicy fish.

When he woke up, on the spot he has a yawn
And then he goes out hunting to find food again.
With joy in his heart, he eats another fish.

Jamie Roxburgh (10)
Comrie Primary School, Comrie

Smoking

Smokers keep going puff, puff, puff,
Breathing in that nasty stuff.
Just wait till their skin turns yellow!
Hear them cough when they bellow.
They started with one and then got hooked!
They'll lose the lovely way they looked.

Regal, Mayfair, Lambert & Butler,
They all came because of Hitler!
4,000 chemicals all mixed up,
Yet their business has not gone corrupt!
It makes a horrible, nasty smell,
Stop it now before you're unwell!

Catherine Payne (10)
Comrie Primary School, Comrie

Stones

Rubies are red like the red, red rose
Sapphires are blue like the blue, blue sky
Emeralds are green like the green, green grass
Topaz are turquoise like the deep, deep sea
Pearls are white like the white, white snow
Diamonds are sparkly like the stars in the sky.

Natalie Moffat (10)
Comrie Primary School, Comrie

Happiness

Yellow as a blazing sun.
Scrumptious as Christmas pudding.
Smells like a sweet banana.
Birthday cake running down my face.
A choir of angels singing, bursting with excitement.

John Clark (7)
Conon Bridge Primary School, Dingwall

Calmness

Multicoloured like a rainbow in a clear blue sky.
Tastes like a sizzling burger
With melted cheese running down the side.
Smells like a bright yellow daffodil
In a fresh green meadow.
A cute koala scurrying up a eucalyptus tree.
The wind rustling through light brown autumn leaves.
Feels like a sparkling stone fresh from a clean and clear river.

Jared De Kruijff (8)
Conon Bridge Primary School, Dingwall

Happiness

Blue like the wide ocean.
Mint ice cream that I have at home with my family.
Smells like pure chocolate.
Looks like a blazing fire.
Birds singing in the trees.
A squiggly balloon that just burst.

Sarah Macdonald (7)
Conon Bridge Primary School, Dingwall

Anger

Dark red like burning fire.
Like hard bread just out of the freezer.
Like sweat running down my face.
Rotten fields that have never been cut.
Like thunder coming down to Earth.
A hard boulder in the quarry.

Shaun Reid
Conon Bridge Primary School, Dingwall

Excitement

White like snow on a crispy winter's day.
Tastes like snowflakes drifting onto my tongue.
Smells like Margerita pizza.
Presents under the Christmas tree.
Santa's bells jingling.
Feels like you're going on an exciting holiday.

Ian Ross (7)
Conon Bridge Primary School, Dingwall

Happiness

As yellow as a yumcious banana
Tastes like crumbling, crusty bread
Lavender perfume
Smiling daisies in my garden
Sounds like tinkling glass
When my dad says congratulations.

Andrew Kyle (7)
Conon Bridge Primary School, Dingwall

Happiness

As pink as icing on a birthday cake,
Tastes like a scrumptious Christmas pudding.
Smells like roses in the garden.
Looks like vanilla ice cream.
Sounds of people laughing.
Feels like a jumping dolphin.

Lewis Mulhearn (8)
Conon Bridge Primary School, Dingwall

Jealousy

Red like blood dripping from Hell.
Like a big juicy apple.
Smells like a pure strawberry.
Smoke from a chimney.
A block of soot sliding down the chimney.
Feels like a blaze of fire heading for the sky.

Logan Sinclair (7)
Conon Bridge Primary School, Dingwall

Jealousy

Red, wet blood dripping
Tastes of sour onions in stew
Smells like farmyard dung
A bolt of lightning hitting the ground
Nails screeching down the blackboard
Feels like a blaze of flame hitting the sky.

Alasdair Williamson (7)
Conon Bridge Primary School, Dingwall

Happiness

As red as sweet lips
Tastes like a lovely chocolate pudding
It smells like roast on a plate
Because it reminds me of my best friend.

Looks like people smiling and grinning
Sounds like lovely songs
Feels like soft rose petals.

Courtney Mackenzie (8)
Conon Bridge Primary School, Dingwall

Happiness

Pink like icing on a birthday cake with seven candles on it.
Tastes like a cherry cake.
Smells like blue cheese on a plate.
Looks like roses coming out of the ground.
Sounds like people singing.
Feels like bursting with laughter.

Calum Cumming (7)
Conon Bridge Primary School, Dingwall

Happiness

Red as the colour of the sky at sunset
Tastes like juicy apple
Smells like fresh daisies
Looks like my silly sister
Feels like sheep's wool.

Callum Russell (7)
Conon Bridge Primary School, Dingwall

Calmness

Light blue like the summer sky.
Tastes like beautiful sweet muffins.
Smells like fresh air.
Looks like clouds high above.
Feels like I am lying on smooth grass.

Neil Cameron (7)
Conon Bridge Primary School, Dingwall

Happiness

A dark red like a red rose.
Tastes like chocolate pudding.
Smells like a fresh, lovely sun.
Looks like Christmas,
Sounds like Mum singing.
Feels like Easter time.

Emily Fouka (8)
Conon Bridge Primary School, Dingwall

Happiness

As red as a juicy red apple,
Tastes like a strawberry dipped in sugar,
Smells like a pie coming out of the oven,
Looks like chocolate ice cream with a cherry on the top,
Sounds like it's the middle of spring,
Feels like a daisy gazing in the sun.

Innes Bushell (8)
Conon Bridge Primary School, Dingwall

Art

Art is a painting
Art is a pot
Art is a skill that some folk forgot.
Art is a picture that sticks in your mind
Art is an art that some people find.
Art is a figure carved from oak
Art is a very elaborate cloak.
Art is the knack of catching fish
Art is no school, oh I wish!

Amy Piggot (11)
Drakies Primary School, Inverness

The House Numbers

Number 1 is a spoil sport,
Number 2 escaped from court.
Number 3 always says *moo!*
Number 4 likes to swim down the loo!
Number 5 is always late,
Number 6 is anything but great.
Number 7 supports Caley Thistle,
Number 8 likes to stab people with his chisel!
Number 9 always cries,
Number 10 always wears his tie.
Number 11 always watches TV,
Number 12 always needs a pee!
Number 13 loves to eat,
Number 14 is a cheat.
Number 15 licks snails,
Number 16 has 100 tails.
Number 17 is really cool,
Number 18 is obsessed with school.
Number 19 breaks all her bones,
Number 20 steals traffic cones.
Number 21 grew a beard,
Number 22 is really weird.
Number 23 is really fat,
Number 24 is obsessed with her cat
And the person who lives in the number of glory,
Is spoilt, rich and never sorry.

Chris Deacon (10)
Drakies Primary School, Inverness

My Castle

I wish I had a castle,
It wouldn't be a hassle.
It would have a swimming pool
And a dog that would drool.
It would have a green,
Cut by a man who was lean.
I would have a cook,
Who would fill my stomach's every nook.
I would have a stable
And a groom who was able.
I would hold a ball,
In a room with a green and white wall
And in the winter nights,
I would watch the boxing fights.
I would stare out the window sill,
Watching my gardener called Bill.
It would have a fountain,
In front of a mountain.
But soon it would sink in,
My real home's the bin.
Of a wonderful castle galore,
Oh if only I had more!

Adam Kelly (10)
Drakies Primary School, Inverness

At The Beach

You can feel the sand between your toes,
As you stumble over rows and rows
Of people lying and getting a tan,
Or cooling themselves with a fluttering fan.
Swimming in the clear blue sea,
Is where you really love to be.
The sun beats down on your burning neck,
As you watch the screeching seagulls peck
At the scraps of people's picnic food,
Thinking it tastes really good.
Beach balls fly all over the place,
As you rub suncream all around your face.
The weather gets colder, people start to leave,
The time has come for your to grieve.
You're on your way home, you start to cry,
You really don't want to say goodbye!

Stacey MacDonald (10)
Drakies Primary School, Inverness

My Dog Fergus

My dog Fergus, he's my pet,
He really absolutely hates the vet!
My dog Fergus, cuddly as a bear,
You should see his brown and golden hair.

My dog Fergus, he's a Yorkie,
He's also a little bit porky!
My dog Fergus is loving and kind
And a mischief mastermind!

My dog Fergus loves to play,
He's the best, the end, OK!

Robbie Lorimer (10)
Drakies Primary School, Inverness

Wildlife

I love to hear the blue tit sing
And see the buzzard use its great big wings,
I love to see the rabbits run into their burrow when they see a fox.

But the sad thing is when you hear a squeal
You will start to snivel.
I love to see the king of all glens
The stag's one of my all time favourites,
The strong and mighty beast.

I love to see the pine martens run up the trees with glee,
I am glad that I'm here to see all these beautiful things today,
But one day I won't so I will enjoy it while I can,
For I will always be the number one wildlife fan.

Sarah Harper (9)
Drakies Primary School, Inverness

My Auntie

My auntie is weird,
She grew a long beard,
It stretches down to her toes!

My auntie is strange,
She's out of the range,
Grey hairs grow out of her nose!

My auntie's out of her mind,
She's the strangest woman you'll find,
People stare wherever she goes!

But the mystery is,
Why my mum's big sis,
Is totally demented and acts like this!

Emma MacAulay (10)
Drakies Primary School, Inverness

Witch's Brew

Put a bit of tail of dog,
Don't forget the legs of frog,
Also put the ear of cat,
Try, try, try the wing of bat.

Pick it up, stir it round,
It will make a lovely sound.

I heard hamsters' eyes taste very nice,
Then also add a bit of mice,
Then put some eye of tiger
And all the bubbles will swoop higher.

Pick it up, stir it round,
It will make a lovely sound.

Don't forget to add to the brew,
Some of the blood and veins of you.

Lesley Barron (10)
Drakies Primary School, Inverness

The Guy Who Walks Around Town

There's this guy who walks around town,
He always has a frown.
He never looks happy,
The guy still wears a nappy.

Then a TV crew from the USA came,
They were looking for someone with fortune and fame.
Then a guy said, 'What about him over there?
He would be perfect for the bear.'

So there you have it all my hopes and dreams thrown away.
Oh well, what a day.

Craig Brand (10)
Drakies Primary School, Inverness

Primary School

Sitting in the boring class,
Staring at the page of maths.
I would rather bake a cake,
I can't wait till break.

Now we have to do some English,
I don't think I'll ever finish!
I can't wait for gym to come
The boy across from me has bitten his tongue.

Maybe history will be better,
Head teacher will come and hand out a letter.
(It's boring no doubt.)

No the pupils are wrong.
The bathrooms are making a pong,
Now we get to stay off school.
All the pupils shout, 'Cool!'

Next time we do French,
I think I'll just dig a trench.
I'm away to Hong Kong,
I know I'll get away from any pong.

Gemma Ross (10)
Drakies Primary School, Inverness

Football

Football is the best game ever,
Out or in I always play it.
Overhead the ball flies,
All the best players do tackles.
Ball was kicked and kicked into the goals,
All the time I never missed a goal.
Lobbed it right into the goals,
Long kick went near the goals and hit the post.

Steven Fraser (10)
Drakies Primary School, Inverness

School

The school breaks up, the school breaks down
I think that it will fall down
It's a good thing can't you see
Soon I will be jumping with glee
I won't have to do more maths
And no more silly old tasks
The cafeteria is filled with sick
Go on have a lick
Kick up the pencils, kick up the rulers
Kick up the pens, kick up the lens
Right that's it I'm off
But before I go there's one more thing I've got to do
Go to the loft and say, 'Switcharoo.'

Alanna Goddard (10)
Drakies Primary School, Inverness

Seasons Are Passing

S pring is snowdrops sprouting everywhere,
E ven daffodils here and there,
A dults are in the park drinking wine,
S ummer is now over and it's autumn time,
O h it's so dull and trees are bare,
N o animals out, not even a hare,
S o it's now winter with Christmas drawing near
But spring will be back some time next year!

Robyn Stark (10)
Drakies Primary School, Inverness

Victorian Schools

Let's go up
Let's go down
Let's go across
To Victorian times.
I want to see how the Victorian schools worked.
Here comes the cane, I get smacked on the hands and on the bum.
Did I do something wrong? Oh yes I did.
I smacked the teacher and dropped the slate.
I didn't stop there, here comes the teacher, oh I don't care.
But who does anyway
I'd rather work with coal.
But not in the tunnel oh no!
I'd throw the coal in the cart,
It's better than my smelly Victorian school.
Up and down, across I go,
Back to the present, that's better now,
Don't you think so?

Leigh-Anne Anderson (10)
Drakies Primary School, Inverness

Sports

S wimming in the
P ool is tiring
O r sometimes boring, the ice
R ink is freezing and
T ennis is fun but
S port is really good for your body so I like
Sport!

Steven Ednie (10)
Drakies Primary School, Inverness

A Witch's Poem

I'm here to brew a poison for you,
I hope you don't mind if I do.
I like to ride on my broom,
I'll pass by and steal the groom.
I like my cat,
I like my hat,
I like a toad, nice and fat.
I once was healthy,
I once was wealthy,
But now I am really stealthy.

Kerry MacDonald (10)
Drakies Primary School, Inverness

Queen Victoria

Queen Victoria had a secret
That she never told.
We looked up, we looked down
But it was never stored.

Some people say it was in her diary.
Some people say, 'No.'
Victorians would say
Have you found her secret yet?
We would shout, 'No!'

Rachel MacDougall (10)
Drakies Primary School, Inverness

Pool

Pool is my favourite sport
It's great in every way.
My dad taught me how to play,
He's a Scottish classic champion
And he knows all the rules
He's really cool and great in every way.
It's hard to pot the balls,
But that's what I do when duty calls.
I always snooker my dad,
He thinks it's really cheeky,
But he always wins 40 out of 40
I will always play
Pool.

Brian Phillips (10)
Drakies Primary School, Inverness

Cooking

Cooking is great fun,
Why not make a bun?
If you like cakes why not try a big one,
If you have a son or daughter
Bring them one of our cakes along.
Can't you see there are no cakes left?
Oh no, I just love cakes
But they can't be all gone!

Lucy Templeton (11)
Drakies Primary School, Inverness

Animals

Animals, animals everywhere,
Monkeys, horses and polar bears.
Zebras, penguins and kangaroos,
All of them are at the zoo.

How about a big scary snake,
It's escaped, *argh!* For goodness sake.
They are all such wonderful creatures,
Each one with their own special feature.

Marc McPherson (10)
Drakies Primary School, Inverness

Monday's Child

Monday's child is tired,
Tuesday's child got fired.
Wednesday's child got hired.
Thursdays' child admired chocolate.
Friday's child is an alcoholic,
Saturday's child is mean and horrible
And the child that was born on the Sabbath day
Isn't good in every way.

Jordan Cooper (10)
Drakies Primary School, Inverness

My Cousin

My cousin needs the potty every afternoon,
He's very spotty and snotty,
He's very naughty so I tell him,
'I'm going to smack your botty.
Your botty will be red so you won't be able to sit down.'
He has brown hair like a fizzy whizzy bear
And doesn't care if he's bare!

Chloe Reid (10)
Drakies Primary School, Inverness

I am Inside Looking Outside

I am inside looking outside
Looking at the sparkling snow as it falls on the ground.
Looking at the very pretty trees covered with snow.
Looking at the swooping leaves blowing in the wind.
Looking at the singing robins singing a pretty tune.
Listening to the screaming children
As they go down very steep icy hills on their sledges.
Looking at the very icy rocks in the shade.
Listening to the whistling wind as it blows and blows.
Looking at the children all wrapped up warm
With their scarves and gloves and hats.
Looking at people going for a walk down the road.
I am inside looking outside, looking at winter.

Monique Hendy (8)
Dunecht School, Westhill

Inside/Outside

I am inside, looking outside,
Listening to the jingling bells.
Watching children putting wreaths on their front door.
Listening to the crunching of wrapping paper.
Watching all the gleaming lights.
Watching the children sleeping in bed.
Watching shadows in the night sky.
Listening to presents rustling and rattling.
Listening to the poor ducks quacking in the frozen ponds.
Watching children put on their mitts and winter hats.
Watching families put lights on the trees.
I am inside looking outside.

Mhairi Cargill (7)
Dunecht School, Westhill

Inside/Outside

I am inside looking outside
Looking at towering igloos
Listening to the cars going by
Making snow tracks
Looking at the children
Sledging down the hills
Looking at children
Building snowmen.
Listening to the ice rattling.
I am inside looking outside
At the snow.

Finlay McPherson (7)
Dunecht School, Westhill

A Snowy Winter

I am inside looking outside
On the twinkling, glistening snow.
Looking at polar bears playing,
Looking at penguins fishing,
Looking at Santa's workshop,
Looking at shining ice.
I am inside looking outside.

Molly Spooner (8)
Dunecht School, Westhill

A Snowy Day

I am inside looking outside
at the falling snow
and the snow's glow.
I am looking at the trees that blow.
I am looking at the children
building snowmen.
I am inside looking outside.

Cameron Brownie (7)
Dunecht School, Westhill

A Winter Fantasy Land

I am inside looking outside
at a snow-frosted hut and carriage
resembling a sugar-frosted
gingerbread house and pumpkins.

I am looking at the glittering, shimmering trees
and the snowflakes dancing in the sunlight.
The sound or robins twittering.
I am inside looking outside at winter.

Kyla Hislop (8)
Dunecht School, Westhill

Before the Red Suit
Came Down The Chimney

I am inside looking outside
I'm looking at the kids rolling on the snowy ground.
I'm looking at the snowy moon.
I'm looking at kids building snowmen.
I'm looking at kids sledging down the snowy hill.
I'm looking at the polar bears fishing.
I'm inside looking outside.

Hayley O'Brien (8)
Dunecht School, Westhill

Inside Outside

I am inside looking outside
Looking at the snow storms blowing everything around.
Looking at the snowmen being built.
Looking at the snowflakes fluttering
Looking at the snow crunching.

Daniel Wilson (7)
Dunecht School, Westhill

Inside Outside

I am inside looking outside
at the beautiful white snow
and people throwing snowballs.
I am inside looking outside
at all the people snowboarding
and some skating.
I am inside looking outside
as all the igloos melt
and all the snow twinkles.

Stephen Will (7)
Dunecht School, Westhill

Winter

I am inside looking outside
I am looking at glistening snowflakes
Falling from the sparkly sky.
I am listening to the lovely little children laughing.
I can smell some fresh crispy air.
I can taste some roasting hot food
I am touching some woolly hats.
I am inside looking outside.

Kerryn McRae (8)
Dunecht School, Westhill

Winter

Looking at the snowmen being built
Looking at the snow crunching
Looking at the children throwing snowballs
Looking at the glittering, shimmering, twinkling snowflakes.

Calum Rae (9)
Dunecht School, Westhill

Inside/Outside

I am inside looking outside
I am looking at the snow
And people playing as their fingers glow.
I am inside looking outside,
I am looking at the snow,
I am looking at ice being swept away by the wind's blow,
I am inside looking outside,
I am looking at the snow,
Watching the snow's level grow.

Kenneth MacBeath (8)
Dunecht School, Westhill

A Snowy Day

I am inside looking outside
Looking at children wearing warm clothes
Looking at the glittering snow falling
Listening to the children laughing
As they sledged down the hills.
Listening to the crackling ice
As it glides down the window.
Looking at the towering igloos
Looking at the children building snowmen.
I am inside looking outside at winter.

Joanna Cook (8)
Dunecht School, Westhill

A Recipe For A Happy New Year

First take some smiles and a handful of sparkling money.
Then scatter in a million happy homes.
Next pinch a cup of kindness and a flower for the world.
Then catch a new sparkling generation
And what do you have?
A happy new year.

Sam Povey (8)
Dunecht School, Westhill

Shadow Knights

The ninja lurks in shadows dark,
Shrinking from shadow to shadow.

He seems to melt into the darkness
Becoming one with it.

He will not take any risks
Waits in the darkest of shadows as a coiled viper.

Ready to pounce on his target
Any way to dispose of him will do.

A drop of poison, swipe of knife,
All these ways shall extinguish his life.

The ninja is sent by rival generals, nobles, kings,
To stealthily assassinate anyone they please.

But if he should fail,
His life is seriously forfeit.

His master, the owner has the will,
To kill the wicked, dishonoured soul.

However if the ninja accomplishes his task,
The emperor shall honour and reveal the face behind the mask.

For these deadly knights of the shadow realm,
Are taught in the darkest of arts.

Their nimble ways, their silent strikes,
Are bred in the depths of the shadows.

Michael Huntington (11)
Dunecht School, Westhill

The Poppy

The heart of the poppy is black
for the men that never came back.
The petals of the poppy are red
for the blood that the soldiers shed.

The people who went and said goodbye
they went and fought and then they died.
The people in town were very sad
then they thought, *what very brave lads.*

People stay silent on the 11th of November
to remember the soldiers that fought and died.
People don't like the destruction of war
for it kills and destroys bodies and minds.

Rachael Will (11)
Dunecht School, Westhill

A Snowy Christmas

I am inside looking outside
I am looking up at the snowy moon
With a dove flying under it
With a four-leaved clover in its mouth.
I see a snowy igloo
It almost looks like a snow globe.
I see the smoky fire
Roaring with my stocking on top.
Looking at children building a snowman
With a big carrot nose.
Seeing a pair of red trousers
Stuck in a chimney.

Hannah Johnston (8)
Dunecht School, Westhill

Transformation

Here I am in my pond, with all my
brothers and sisters.

I am swimming inside my egg,
singing and dancing to my heart's content.

Here I am in my pond, bigger now
and transformed.
I have a tail and a small head
the next step is ahead.

Here I am in my pond
I've grown four legs
and lost my tail,
my transformation has not failed.
Here I am, now a frog,
I'm thinking of moving to a nice wet bog.

James Huntington (9)
Dunecht School, Westhill

Clara

Unusual, black and white
My four-legged friend Ciara.

Jumping, running, darting,
Fun-loving Ciara.

Soft and cuddly, warm and snuggly,
My loving companion Ciara.

Obedient, kind, energetic, caring,
Incredibly cute collie dog . . .
Ciara.

Christopher Huntington (9)
Dunecht School, Westhill

Under My Bed

Under my bed there are wonderful things,
Like spiders and cobwebs and missing earrings
And I'm sad to say that my mum said,
'Throw out that junk that's under your bed!'

So I stuck my head under to take a look
And I started to laugh and I laughed till I shook.
What on Earth would Mum say,
Cos down there are my pants from yesterday.

My laughing has stopped,
This is gross, I think,
Because here's an old sock
That practically stinks!

But worse than that,
All safely tucked up,
Was a mouldy old sandwich,
Now it's time to say *yuck!*

Oh gosh, oh golly,
I'll be in trouble for this,
For here is the homework,
From a week that I missed.

Shona MacBeath (11)
Dunecht School, Westhill

Fear

Fear is black
Fear tastes sour
Fear smells like burning rubber
Fear looks like dead flowers
Fear sounds like screaming
Fear feels like being hit.

Aaron Brown (9)
Dunecht School, Westhill

Evolution

All fours on the ground
Leaning on his hands
Slowly, slowly stretching up
Over millions of years.

First his hands rise from the ground
Not resting on his knuckles any more
The only communication made
Is a string of loud grunts.

Then be begins to stand upright
On his two medium sized feet
Now he stands tall and straight
Starting to communicate.

Later he is losing all his hair
Only little bits left here and there.

Now he is a man standing tall,
Walking on the Earth
He looks at the water and sees his reflection
And does not know how much he has changed.

Shona Thompson (11)
Dunecht School, Westhill

Nature's Nonsense

Nature is a funny thing
It could show up anywhere
In the water or in a hole.
You could be eaten by a polar bear
Or swallowed by a crocodile
Or even pecked by a woodpecker.
No matter who it is nature will jump up on anyone,
Even you.

Kieran Brown (10)
Dunecht School, Westhill

What's There?

I wonder what's under the bed?
Maybe there's a monster,
Waiting for me!

I wonder what's under the bed?
Maybe there's a ghost,
Waiting for me!

I wonder what's under the bed?
Maybe it's a giant spider,
Waiting to haunt me!

I wonder what's under the bed?
I think it's my imagination,
Trying to scare me!

Caitlin Drummond (9)
Dunecht School, Westhill

My Brave Son

I said goodbye to my beloved child,
Who I might not ever see again,
Never to smile, or to stand,
In front of me again.

My brave little boy,
Who went to war,
To die in poppy fields,
The poppy red as the blood my soldier boy shed,
The black echoes my grief,
Loved and we will be loved,
Now he lies in peace in Flanders field.

Stephanie Jane Malcolm (11)
Dunecht School, Westhill

D-Day

I believe I've done my bit by fighting
Both the Jerries and the Japs.
But now I've to do one more thing
By landing on the Normandy sands.

At the moment we are in the boat
We're heading for the shore.
The 101 Airborne Brigade
Are the spearhead of the force.

The German guns are firing
Upon our bonny boat.
Leaving great holes in her hull
And scarring her blue paint-work.

Then the carrier door falls open
And we rush onto the sand.
There was an almighty eruption
As my men had stepped on the mines.

My men ran for the shelter
Of the bunker not far away.
But we could still see all the bullets
Whipping towards the sea.

Finally the reinforcements come
We storm the bunkers and the hill.
And then the Jerries surrendered
But we lost many good brave men.

So now we all remember
That sad and desperate day.
When the British, French and Americans
Gave their lives away.

Angus Wood (11)
Dunecht School, Westhill

A City In The Clouds

There's a city in the clouds,
Shrouded in mist.
On a little hilltop,
Far in the abyss.
Where the sun never shines
And the moon dominates,
There's a boy on the hill,
Waiting beside the gate.
How did he get there?
No one will know.
Where is he going?
Only time will show.
The gate it opens,
Out comes the light.
Shining so brightly,
Through the dark, misty night.
The boy he enters the city,
So strong and so bold
And there he feels better,
For no longer is he cold.
His family are waiting,
With tears in their eyes
And the boy he jumps,
For he is surprised.
The gate it closes,
With a mighty crack,
In the night so misty
And oh so black.

Cameron Spooner (10)
Dunecht School, Westhill

Poor To Famous

In the horrible times of
World War II,
On the 25th of April,
A boy named Gus was born,
Into a very poor family indeed.

He was loved very much
By his mum and dad
And adored by his older sister.
But when poor Gus was only five,
His dear parents died together
And his beloved sister was
Taken to a prisoner of war camp.

Poor Gus was on his own for many a year,
But one day a man heard
Him singing a sad song.
It was about his parents
But the man was very impressed!

He took Gus to a famous writer,
To beg him to write a letter
To a man in London,
Who did hear Gus' voice
And did make Gus a true star!

For the rest of his life
Gus was rich and strong
And sang lots of different songs,
But almost all of them
Were for his dear parents,
Whose deaths he would never forget,
And his beloved sister
Whom he had never again met.

So, a boy who was born very poor,
Grew up to be a rich and famous star,
He will never forget his two lives,
One good, one bad, one poor, one rich,
And the family he so dearly loved.

Rhea Shearer (9)
Dunecht School, Westhill

In The Blue

Angler fish have lights on their heads,
They also have lots of fears and dreads,
The blue whale is the ocean's biggest creature,
While the Titanic is just a feature.

The ocean blue spreads far and wide,
You have to watch out for the tide,
It might take a while to explore the sea,
So mind to take a flask of tea.

A pillow on the ocean's bed,
Would be a good rest for your head,
You would wake up with surrounding fish,
You would feel like food in a dish,
You can swim as much as you like,
Because you're in the open and there's no dyke.

If you have a boat, explore the sea,
You could be just like me,
The ocean is an awesome place,
You are invited to an ocean race.

I am shattered why could that be?
I don't have the energy to climb a tree.
Can you help me find a treasure chest?
I can't wait for my long desired rest.

Simon O'Brien (11)
Dunecht School, Westhill

First Week At School

My first day at school
There were quite a lot of people.
It was scary in a way,
'Cause P7s they looked lethal.

My second day at school
Wasn't as good as the first.
I got all my sums wrong in maths
And the teacher almost burst.

My third day at school
I made a very good friend.
I didn't think that friendship like this,
Would ever, ever end.

My fourth day at school
We had Brussels sprouts for lunch.
We moaned and we groaned to the teacher
As she said,
'I've never heard such a very noisy bunch.'

My fifth day at school
Was a good bit better,
The teacher thought I did well today,
But on her desk was a big brown letter.

My first weekend from school
My friend came to play.
We played a game of schools and teachers,
Well, what more can you say?

Naomi Pearson (11)
Dunecht School, Westhill

What Is Harvest?

Harvest is when the crops are all cut,
You can see squirrels going out to get a nut,
The farmers are combining all the fields,
Hoping to do better than last year's yield.

Chopping barley, oats and wheat,
Needed the rain and the heat,
Strawberries, raspberries are ready to pick,
They make very fine jam, mmm can I have a lick?

Leaves are falling off the trees,
When there is a very strong breeze,
Autumn is coming fast and strong,
That's why the birds sing a different song.
Thank you.

Donna McGinley (10)
Dunecht School, Westhill

My Son

I waved my son away that day
Thinking he would never pass away
I did not dream of him to die
That day, I said goodbye.

In the trenches, oh so red
People don't know, the blood they shed,
The honours, the pain, of that awful place,
He kept on dreaming, of his mother's face.

He will never grow old,
For that day he was so bold,
He now lies in peace,
For us to remember.

Rachel May Johnston (11)
Dunecht School, Westhill

To A Cheetah

O' what a fluffy cheetah ye are,
I know ye are fast and furious,
But I am a bit curious about ye,
Ye have got big sharp teeth,
So I will watch out,
So ye dinna bite me.

I'm just a person so don't harm me please
Ye can hae some peas
Or if ye prefer ye can hae a bee
An' if ye are thirsty ye can hae a cup o' tea.

Ye are a very roaring cheetah
Ye hunt all ower town
For some good food and maybe a human now and then
If he's very hungry an' lucky.

Natasha Anderson (11)
East End Primary School, Elgin

Tae Nessie

Whit ye up tae ye scary beast?
Thy waiting for a yummy feast
A bird is what ye wad hae at least
Thy art a mystery to the world
No one knows where you hide
But Loch Ness is where you bide.

People come to hae a look
They've even written ye in a book
Many times people tried to catch ye wi a hook
But ye survived.

Raye Hannah
East End Primary School, Elgin

Tae A Blackbird

We saw ye flop o' the tree,
Poor helpless bird that's oh so wee,
Thee canna fly ye poor wee thing,
We guessed ye had a broken wing.

Jole we named ye,
And put ye in a cage wi'
A blanket and some food,
Ye seemed in quite a good mood.

Ye shortly died and we buried ye,
We wept for the poor bird that's wee,
Me guessed you wasn't that wild
Thy poor we body must hae been cauld.

Lauren Ford (11)
East End Primary School, Elgin

To A Horse

Ye bonnie horse so big and brown,
Ye look so proud like yer wearing a crown,
Ye a running and working beast,
I lay ye hay for you to feast,
Ye must be strong to pull a plough,
Ye must get up, it's to work now.

Yer out in the field on a day so cold,
Yer the best horse on the job or so I am told,
Yer just so obedient and oh bold,
Ye best work hard or the land shall be sold,
Horse go and work yer best,
After ye can hae a rest.

Matthew Tulip (11)
East End Primary School, Elgin

Tae A Ghostie

O' where ye hiding ye scary ghostie
Do ye mak the weather so cold and frosty?
Why do ye jump out and give everyone a scare
Nobody really thinks it's fair.

Are ye really white or are ye clear?
We don't know if ye are far or near
Are ye tall or are ye sma'?
Why do ye push people down and mak' them fa'?

Did ye used to live in here?
Did anyone ever come near?
What kind o' food do ye like?
What about fish there's a fish called pike.

Why when ye go tae sleep
Ye always lie and weep and weep?
Are ye a girl or are ye a boy?
Is thy name David, Tom or Roy?

Sarah Mills (11)
East End Primary School, Elgin

To A Spider

Far ye guan ya wee beastie
Dinna be scared
Far ye now ya sm'thing
Oh there ya are!

Now whare ye guan ya creepy beastie
Ye hae eight wee eyes and eight wee legs
Ye scare me much more than I scare thee.

Ta ta wee beastie
Go afore I squish thee
Ya wee scary beastie.

Ross McGillivaray (11)
East End Primary School, Elgin

Tae A Fishy!

Tae ye' ugly rotten fishy,
Sat upon ma' poor dog's dishy,
Fae the river tae the bowl,
Ma' wee dogs gonna eat ye' up whole.

When he sa' ye' he ran tae the plate,
Sorry wee fishy it's a bit tae late,
We swept ye' up fae the river,
Cut oot all ye' guts and liver.

I've never forgotten ye' were a bit tae rotten,
An' stank oot the house a' day,
But by the way ma' dog thought ye',
Were tasty!
Next time wee fishy dinna be hasty.

Samantha Tonberg (11)
East End Primary School, Elgin

To A Dog

Oh ye are a wee beastie
Ye live in my housie
Ye have so sharp teeth
Ye can bite a thief
As ye wait by the stable
Ye can't wait until yer by the table.

When you eat yer meal
Ye get fatter and fatter
Ye wish you were a seal
Ye love chasing cats
An' you lay on the mats.

Robert Mouncher (11)
East End Primary School, Elgin

Tae A Fish

Whare ye gaun ya wee wee fishie
I'll catch ya an put thee on my dishie
You'll wriggle awa thee wishie thee wishie.
I'll rig oot thy gut an cut off thy heid
Once I do this thee will be deid.

I'll cuik ye in a cookin' pot
I said to my brither you'll like it a lot
You lucky wee fishie I didn't leave ye to rot
Although I gave it a lot of thought.

Everyone said it was really nice
We ate ye wi' some tasty rice
Well that's me done wie thee wee fishie
Fish is now my favourite dishie.

Calum Leiper (11)
East End Primary School, Elgin

Tae A Tiger

O' ye big stripy beastie,
How ye wad like tae eat my breastie.
When ye run past me very fast,
I tak a net so vast.
Then I shout, 'Come back here!'
Wi' which I shout with lots of fear.

When I daur try tae catch you,
I try tae find out what ye do.
When ye eat ye food,
It looks very good.
I'm glad I'm nae ye meal,
Just imagine how I'd feel.

Staci Smith (12)
East End Primary School, Elgin

Capture

I want to capture the sound of birds singing a beautiful
song in the trees.

I want to capture the feel of sea creatures swimming past
me in the water.

I want to capture the smell of delicious food ready to eat.

I want to capture the taste of ice cream melting in my mouth.

I want to capture the moment when I walked into Old Trafford
and saw all the players.

I want to capture the memory of my eighth birthday party
when I went bowling and got a strike.

I want to capture the silence of the countryside on
a lovely sunny day.

I want to capture the excitement on Christmas Eve as
I wait for Santa.

Darren Mair (10)
East End Primary School, Elgin

Tae A Cat

Hey ye wee furry cat,
Don't you daur jump on my mat,
Why don't ye search this rotten house
Tae see if ye can see a mouse?

If ye canna find a mouse,
Why don't ye jump in some other person's house,
Bit the man wi the pipe micht kick ye richt out
Wi the toe of his big black boot.

Kristoffer McKenzie (11)
East End Primary School, Elgin

Capture

I want to capture the sounds of
Angels singing in the clouds above.
I want to capture the feel of a melting
Iceberg as the water drips down.
I want to capture the smell of the salty sea
As the tide comes in.
I want to capture the sight of sea animals
When I'm walking underwater.
I want to capture the taste of candyfloss
Melting in my mouth.
I want to capture the moment when I can fly
Like a bird in the sky.
I want to capture the memory of me walking
On the moon some day.
I want to capture the silence of a book
Opening and closing.
I want to capture the feeling of excitement
As I float and explore in space.

Allan Watt (10)
East End Primary School, Elgin

Tae A Dog

Hey ye hairy sleverin' beastie,
I've got to say you smell the leastie,
Ye bark and woof a' the day,
If anybody touches you they will pay.

Ye chase the cat around the park,
Ye chase him round till after dark,
O' a' the animals ye are the best,
Ye beat a' o' them a' the rest.

Francesca Boyes (11)
East End Primary School, Elgin

Capture

I want to capture the sound of bluebells
Shaking off the raindrops.
I want to capture the feel of fluffy white snow
Crunching beneath my feet.
I want to capture the smell of chocolate
Melting in a glass bowl.
I want to capture the sight of a rainbow
With a pot of gold at either end.
I want to capture the taste of the sugary
Icing on my birthday cake dissolving in my mouth.
I want to capture the moment when we stepped
Out of the car onto a beautiful, golden, sandy beach.
I want to capture the memory of my first straight dive like an arrow.
I want to capture the silence of the colourful leaves
Dropping off the trees in autumn.
I want to capture the feeling of my heart beating
Excitedly as I am waiting for a surprise.

Cameron Porter (10)
East End Primary School, Elgin

Tae A Scotsman!

Oh wit strong hairy legs ye hae,
Tae swim in the Loch Nessie,
Ye show off yer legs and get a pay,
Ye swirl and twirl thy kilt sae fine,
Then ye take the ladies oot tae dine.

Ye lift up yer kilt way ower thy heed,
The ladies they will stare indeed,
The tartan on yer kilt is sae good,
Yer job is cuttin' wood,
But boy can that put ye in a good mood.

Fiona Meinen (11)
East End Primary School, Elgin

Capture

I want to capture the sound of wood chimes
Fluttering in the breeze.
I want to capture the sight of salmon jumping
Up the river in search of a new home.
I want to capture the feel of salt sea water
Flowing through my fingers.
I want to capture the smell of a bakery
While they bake fresh bread for me.
I want to capture the moment when I have
My first day of high school.
I want to capture the taste of hot cross buns
At Easter time.
I want to capture the silence of children
Working hard in a classroom.
I want to capture the darkness in a blind person's life.
I want to capture the memory of the world
When it is peaceful forever.

Katrina McIntosh (10)
East End Primary School, Elgin

To A Horsey

Ye bit fat brown horsey
Yer fast asleep in the stable
Laying snoring in the hay
Ye should be working to get yer pay
Wake up now and get to work
So ye can tak us to the kirk
Yer big long legs and yer heavy hooves,
When you're runnin' around on the loose.

Chloe O'Hare (12)
East End Primary School, Elgin

Capture

I want to capture the sound of
Snow falling quietly onto the ground.
I want to capture the feel of a
Fluffy white cat as I stroke it.
I want to capture the smell of the
Sea sparkling in the sun.
I want to capture the sight of fans
Cheering for their favourite team.
I want to capture the taste of bacon
Sizzling in the pan.
I want to capture the moment when
I won a singing competition in Spain.
I want to capture the memory of my grandfather's
Smiling face and bring it to life again.
I want to capture the silence of my fish
Swimming in the pond.
I want to capture the feeling of happiness
I get when I win awards.

Emma McLennan (10)
East End Primary School, Elgin

It Could Have Been . . .

Last night I heard a sound,
It could have been a spider whispering in my ear,
It could have been the fridge humming to itself,
It could have been a leprechaun giggling with glee,
It could have been an angel singing in the sky,
It could have been my toys coming alive to play games,
But it was only my cat scratching at my curtains.

Blossom McAfee (10)
East End Primary School, Elgin

Capture

I want to capture the sound of whales talking to each other
in the deep blue world under the sea.

I want to capture the feel of a large black creature
that nobody has captured before.

I want to capture the smell of blossom at the beginning of spring
and keep it for myself.

I want to capture the sight of a dolphin jumping through the sun
as it sets.

I want to capture the taste of a fresh chocolate cake that has just
been taken out of the oven.

I want to capture the moment when the sun rises
and a new day begins.

I want to capture the memory of my great grandfather
when he was healthy and make sure it lasts forever.

I want to capture the silence of the wind as it blows
quietly through the branches of the trees.

I want to capture the feeling of excitement as I explore a
world unknown to mankind.

Leanne Tonge (10)
East End Primary School, Elgin

Capture

I want to capture the sound of people
Shouting loudly and put it under my bed.

I want to capture the feel of my dad hugging
Me every time I am sad.

I want to capture the smell of my brother's
Feet and lock it away!

I want to capture the sight of aliens and
Show the world that they exist.

I want to capture the taste of chocolate
And keep it on my tastebuds forever.

I want to capture the moment when I cheer
On my cousin running a race and he wins.

I want to capture the memory of winning
A race on sports day.

I want to capture the silence when peace
Is declared all over the world.

I want to capture the feeling of happiness
I have when I visit my dad.

Daniel Harrison (10)
East End Primary School, Elgin

Capture

I want to capture the sound of the wind blowing the leaves
on the ground.
I want to capture the feel of the sea crashing on the rocks.
I want to capture the smell of flowers in the cool breeze.
I want to capture the sight of the lighthouse flashing
to let ships know the rocks are there.
I want to capture the taste of chocolate melting in my mouth.
I want to capture the moment when I started school
and I met my friends.
I want to capture the memory of building a sandcastle on the beach
with my sister.
I want to capture the feeling of silence of the wind blowing in my ear.
I want to capture the feeling of happiness when my friends
tickle me.

Mark Stitt (11)
East End Primary School, Elgin

Capture

I want to capture the sound of a woodpecker pecking on a tree.
I want to capture the feel of snowflakes falling from the sky.
I want to capture the smell of the baker's fresh bread as I walk past.
I want to capture the sight of the sun rising in the sky.
I want to capture the taste of home-made toffee
                    dissolving in my mouth.
I want to capture the moment when I saw four deer in the darkness
                    sleeping under the stars.
I want to capture the memory of my very first snowy white Christmas.
I want to capture the silence of children working very hard in class.
I want to capture the feeling of butterflies in my tummy just before
                    I perform in a play.

Sarah Anderson (10)
East End Primary School, Elgin

Nissan Skyline GTR

Open the door and in I go,
It's my Nissan Skyline with blue glow.
Start the engine, rev it up loud,
My car's illegal and is not allowed.

Wait for the signal, bright glowing green,
I'll be going so fast I won't be seen.
With my callipers and NOS,
Fuel injected turbo and you will guess.

Going faster than TVR and Ferraris together,
The interior is made with real leather.
Onto the dyno, BHP is 990,
Press the numbers and they all say *oh*.

Going faster than Concorde flying low,
Beat Santa Claus saying, 'Ho, ho, ho.'
The drawbridge is raising,
Strangers will hopefully be gazing.

I hope I land the death drop,
Or even hit and trash the New Look shop.
I won the spring race today,
My scanners pick up police, hooray!

I get to race again once more,
I've done a wheel spin into the Earth's core,
They'll never catch me, *hee, hee, hee,*
I'm in sixth gear, it's easy to get away.

I've got a Mini from the street,
It's parked against the wall, I must retreat,
I'll get my car tomorrow
I will be full of sorrow!

Steven Webster (11)
East End Primary School, Elgin

The Ongoing Household

Clocks are chiming
Mum's singing a song
Children miming
All day long!

Shouting, shouting everywhere
Now something's wrong
Tom can't find his underwear
All day long!

It's a snowy day
The doorbell goes *ding-dong*
It's Dad - his name's Ray
All day long!

I'm putting the hammer back in the shed
Don't you shout at me!
Now they're safely tucked in bed
Phew, now I've got time for a cup of tea!

Hannah Scott (11)
East End Primary School, Elgin

Rhyme Chime

There was a man his name was Sam
He lived in Japan with a frying pan.
He set off to space without a case
And his friend said, 'Don't race.'

He landed on Mars, there were no cars
He said, 'I can make a Mars bar.'
He got a flag and stuck it in the ground
And moved around.
But it was nowhere to be found.

So he set off to Earth.
'Finally I can get two years' peace
Without my dog barking in my ears.'

So two years later he landed on Earth
There were people crowding him.
There were some that were proud of him
His family cuddled him and the dog licked him.

Craig Ferguson (10)
East End Primary School, Elgin

The Cheetah

They run as fast as the speed of light
Their big black paws take off with fight
Their coloured spots I can see
I'd better hurry up or he'll catch me!

There's a hunter coming to catch him
I'd better run and go and tell him,
But it doesn't matter because he can run
Way much faster than a bullet from a gun!

He slides past the trees, the river and the bees
I'm surprised he doesn't get sore knees.
I heard a strange cry, has the hunter got him?
No way that can't happen!

We're at his funeral the next day,
I can't believe this has happened, why this way?
He was such a cheery cheetah all the time
The last thing he ate was a little green lime.

Claire Grant (11)
East End Primary School, Elgin

Going Into Space

Astronauts leave their base
They go in the rocket
To try to find an alien race
One of the astronauts
Put his hand in his pocket.

He pulled out some gum
The rocket took off in the air
As that happened he wondered if the aliens
Would be friendly or if they would dare.

He sat down tight to his chair
He saw the planet glitter and spark
It felt like the rocket moved at the speed of light
It was bitterly cold
He stepped on the planet
He and I wondered if we would get back alive.

Allan Slapp (11)
East End Primary School, Elgin

Animal Poem

Hungry shark hunting for his dinner
Deadly shark chasing after me
Puzzled shark swimming round in circles
Grinning shark whose teeth are sharp and pointy
Sniffing shark smelling fresh blood
Brave shark taking over a new territory
Dirty shark shaking all the mud off
Caring shark looking after its babies
Tired shark resting all through the night.

Samantha Watson (9)
Grantown Primary School, Grantown-On-Spey

The Cat

Playful cat rolling on her back.
Hungry cat staring into its empty bowl.
Happy cat purring and licking me.
Scared cat with her hackles up.
Angry cat biting and scratching me.
Wild cat hunting mice and birds.
Lazy cat sleeping all day.
Clumsy cat falling off her scratching post.
Noisy cat miaowing all night.
Caring cat licking her kittens.
Exploring cat running behind the sofa.

Maisie Crake (9)
Grantown Primary School, Grantown-On-Spey

Animal Poem

Golden puppy racing after me
Sad puppy sulking in her bed
Graceful puppy chasing after the ball
Scared puppy hiding behind the bed
Lazy puppy waiting to play
Fast puppy running beside me
Happy puppy waiting for her food
Jumping puppy playing with me
Playful puppy licking me.

Kodie White (8)
Grantown Primary School, Grantown-On-Spey

My Puppy

Happy puppy sitting on my knee
Panting puppy out of breath from running
Cute puppy cuddling into me
Brown-headed puppy, fat, white body,
Little brown legs
Lonely puppy crying in his bed
Small puppy walking in the park
Angry puppy pulling on his lead
Naughty puppy chasing birds
Noisy puppy yapping loudly
Playful puppy with soft toys,
My puppy and me.

Ryan Grant (9)
Grantown Primary School, Grantown-On-Spey

Animal Poem

Brown rabbit sniffing beside the road,
Short rabbit tails bobbing happily,
Cute rabbits licking its paws,
Fast rabbits jumping through the fences,
Mothering rabbit cleaning her kittens,
Lazy rabbit eating grass,
Jumping rabbit crossing the road,
Happy rabbit springing everywhere,
Tired rabbit sleeping in its burrow,
Sad, sulky rabbit hiding in its hole,
Hyperactive rabbit jumping everywhere.

James Coutts (9)
Grantown Primary School, Grantown-On-Spey

Sea Lion

Black sea lion jumping in hoops
Fast sea lion splashing with his fins
Smelly sea lion not wanting a bath
Greedy sea lion eating all the fish
Happy sea lion diving under the sea
Shiny sea lion sitting on the rocks
Clever sea lion balancing a ball on his nose
Proud sea lion clapping his fins.

Lauren Garside (9)
Grantown Primary School, Grantown-On-Spey

My Pet Dog, Sting

Scary dog barking at the window.
Greedy dog eating all the biscuits.
Happy dog bouncing along the road.
Joyful dog playing with me.
Patient dog waiting for his food.
Fluffy dog just been combed.

Hayley McFarlane (9)
Grantown Primary School, Grantown-On-Spey

My Beautiful Dogs

Cute dogs running around
Fast dogs running like the wind
Shining dogs that have just been washed
Happy dogs after they're fed
Graceful dogs every day
Black dogs near and far
Jumping as high as the sky.

James Towers (9)
Grantown Primary School, Grantown-On-Spey

Monkey

Cute monkey playing with me
Bad monkey biting me
Hungry monkey eating all the bananas
Lazy monkey mostly sleeping all day
Silly monkey pulling faces at people
Lively monkey swinging from tree to tree
Happy monkey smiling at me
Jumping monkey breaking all the branches
Cheeky monkey hitting me.

Sarah Grant (9)
Grantown Primary School, Grantown-On-Spey

My Working Dogs

Black dogs fetching the pheasants.
Fast dogs running after the rabbits.
Clever dogs hunting deer.
Happy dogs wandering around.
Quiet dogs in the back of the Land Rover.
Sad dogs howling in the kennel.
Fun dogs playing with me.

Joe Hopkins (9)
Grantown Primary School, Grantown-On-Spey

Animal Poem

Brown horse galloping fast across the fields.
Happy horse trotting over to me.
Hungry horse eating crunchy hay and wavy grass.
Jumping horse in a race going over fences.
Helpful horse carrying people home.

Megan Grant (9)
Grantown Primary School, Grantown-On-Spey

Animal Poem

Blue dolphin swimming through the waves
Graceful dolphin playing by the ship
Fast dolphin swimming under the sea
Strong dolphin carrying people
Clever dolphin swimming through hoops
Smart dolphin dodging the sharks
Dirty dolphin rolling on rocks
Quick dolphin eating fast fish
Nice dolphin looking at me
Good dolphin sparkling in the sunlight
Beautiful dolphin in the shallow water
Mad dolphin kicking the sand
Proud dolphin clapping its fins!

Alexandrea Macleod (9)
Grantown Primary School, Grantown-On-Spey

Animal Poem

Hungry chimp eating big yellow bananas, yummy!
Hungry, noisy chimp with chattering teeth,
Chatter, chatter, chatter!
Hungry, noisy, cheeky chimp making faces, ha, ha, ha!
Hungry, noisy, cheeky, silly chimp tripping over stones,
Crash, bang, wallop!
Hungry, noisy, cheeky, silly, long armed chimp
Swinging on the branches, swoosh, swosh, swing!
Hungry, noisy, cheeky, silly, long armed, gripped feet chimp
Hanging upside down like a bat.
Hungry, noisy, cheeky, silly, long armed, gripped feet
Loony chimp with googly eyes, wooo!

Ruairidh Murray (9)
Grantown Primary School, Grantown-On-Spey

Animal Poem

Fluffy, scary, black dog sniffing people,
Bouncy and fast dog waiting to be played with,
Shiny and brown dog pushing me around,
Mad, biting dog about to kill,
Nice, happy dog licking me like mad,
Brown dog stealing all the biscuits,
Crazy dog running backwards and forwards,
Helpful dog guarding the house,
Bad dog ripping rabbits apart,
Fun dog chasing after me,
Scared dog hiding behind me,
Wet dog soaking me,
Gentle dog sitting beside me
Wise dog choosing to be good
Dirty dog making a mess,
Sad dog crying his heart out,
Sleepy dog sleeping like a baby.
            Sshhh!

Rosie Lean (9)
Grantown Primary School, Grantown-On-Spey

Lion Poem

Angry lion roaring at the tourists
Hungry lion catching her prey
Happy lion playing with the cubs
Bad lion biting me
Mummy lion protecting her cubs
Dizzy lion running in circles
Dirty lion rolling in mud
Lazy lion sleeping quietly (shh)
Soft lion rubbing against me
Beautiful lion looking in the sun
Bleeding lion fighting over a female
Scared lion hiding in his den.

Adam Young (9)
Grantown Primary School, Grantown-On-Spey

An Animal Poem

Blue dolphin swimming beside a ship
Unhappy dolphin swimming by herself
Mother dolphin protecting her young
Graceful dolphin racing through hoops
Joyful dolphin eating fish
Clever dolphin jumping fast over rocks
Sparkling dolphin splashing through the waves
Happy dolphin smiling at me.

Jessie Jones (9)
Grantown Primary School, Grantown-On-Spey

T-Rex

Brown T-rex blending in with trees
Hungry T-rex eating mushy peas
That T-rex is chasing you and me
Clumsy T-rex falling in the sea
That T-rex is good at literature
How did that T-rex draw that picture?
Huge T-rex swishing his tail
No T-rex can open mail!

Greg Lawrence (9)
Grantown Primary School, Grantown-On-Spey

Bull

Bad bull charging at me
Silly bull running into the fence
Angry bull flipping his food about
Upset bull knocking over his bowl of water
Sleepy bull dozing in the sun
Fat bull trying to squeeze through the gate.

Iain Mackellar (9)
Grantown Primary School, Grantown-On-Spey

Deer Poem

Shy deer hiding in the trees
Lazy deer sleeping in the field
Sad deer all alone in a den
Brown deer spotting a female
Scared deer darting through the grass
Fast deer running from dogs
Greedy deer eating all the bark
Kind deer feeding his family.

Adam Finlayson (9)
Grantown Primary School, Grantown-On-Spey

The Squirrel

Bushy squirrel climbing up a tree trunk
Fast squirrel jumping from tree to tree
Cute squirrel nibbling nuts
Sleepy squirrel resting in her nest
Hunting squirrel ready to hibernate
Furry squirrel having fun
Red squirrel looking at me.

Rebecca Amphlett (9)
Grantown Primary School, Grantown-On-Spey

Black Bear

Roaring bear frightening people away
Furry bear all nice and fuzzy
Clumsy bear stuck between the bush
Good bear getting fish for its cubs
Angry bear all tired out
Black bear climbing a tree.

Markus Ruettimann (9)
Grantown Primary School, Grantown-On-Spey

Spider Dog

Very fast dog chasing rabbits and deer
Hungry dog eating dog food and pigs' ears
Fluffy, big, black and hairy dog
High jumping dog jumping over fences
Sniffing dog smelling for food
Lonely dog sitting by himself
Sleepy dog sleeping on his bed
Sad dog howling in his kennel.

Gregor Samuels (9)
Grantown Primary School, Grantown-On-Spey

Titian Kangaroo

Happy kangaroo bouncing like a ball.
Titian kangaroo sleeping in the shade.
Silly baby kangaroo looking out of his pouch.
Mother kangaroo hopping across Australia.
Hungry kangaroo searching for his dinner.
Hot kangaroo exhausted from jumping.
Lazy kangaroo!

Dean Morrison (9)
Grantown Primary School, Grantown-On-Spey

My Duck

Quacky duck swimming round and round
Sad duck sitting all alone
Careful duck following one after one
Happy duck playing peek-a-boo
Lovely duck cuddling me
Angry duck quacking at me
Mother duck looking after her ducklings
Playful duck talking to you.

Gemma Beckwith (9)
Grantown Primary School, Grantown-On-Spey

Monkeys

Brown monkey browsing in the trees.
Fancy monkey flying through the trees
Playful monkey playing tag
Clever monkey catching leaves
Greedy monkeys looking for grubs
Happy monkey hoping for bananas
Splashing monkeys playing in a pool.

Abigail Lavers (9)
Grantown Primary School, Grantown-On-Spey

Dolphin Poem

Beautiful dolphin gleaming in the sun
Happy dolphin jumping up in the air
Playful dolphin eating shiny salmon
Jumping dolphin in and out of the round hoops
Clever dolphin carrying people on its back
Hungry dolphin waiting for food
Friendly dolphin playing with me
Tired dolphin squeaking, *night, night.*

Dayna McWhirter (9)
Grantown Primary School, Grantown-On-Spey

Killer Whale Poem

Black and white killer whale diving beneath the waves
Shining killer whale jumping through hoops
Smooth killer whale carrying people on his nose
Huge killer whale waving his tail
Tired killer whale sleeping all night
Quiet killer whale sneaking on his prey
Tame killer whale letting people pat it
Lonely killer whale swimming round and round.

Alex Donaldson (9)
Grantown Primary School, Grantown-On-Spey

Wild Lizard

Colourful lizard popping its head out of its house.
Energetic lizard zooming through the desert.
Tired lizard all puffed out.
Smiling lizard looking after his family.
Clever lizard sneaking up on its prey.
Kind lizard feeding its family.
Snarling lizard protecting its family from danger.
Lonely lizard in a sulk.
Friendly lizard loving its family.

Jamie McWilliam (9)
Grantown Primary School, Grantown-On-Spey

Animal Poem

Happy duck waddling on the shore
Lost duck knocking on your door
A live duck walking up a hill
A dead duck lying there still
White duck like snow can be
Funny duck playing in the sea
Daffy Duck driving a car
Drunk duck drinking in a bar
Fat duck falling from the air
Shaving duck losing all his hair.

Douglas Hay (9)
Grantown Primary School, Grantown-On-Spey

Golfing

Get your club and get your ball
Don't do this in a hall.
Hit it too hard
You might get banned.

Put your clubs on a rack
To win, don't hold back.
Swing your club, back and forth
Make sure you don't end up thirty-fourth.

Get a hole in one
You have almost won.
Get a huge break of sweat
It's not over yet.

Douglas Peter (8)
Greenloaning Primary School, Dunblane

Vehicles

There are big ones
Medium ones
Some just right for me
Black, red or blue ones
I think they're all cool
But trucks will do for me!
Monster trucks with big wheels
As tall as a tree
Revving engines
Crushing cars
So watch out for me!

Jordan Reilly (9)
Greenloaning Primary School, Dunblane

David Beckham

D avid Beckham is very famous
A mazing at free kicks
V alued by England and Real Madrid
I ndefinitely a brill football player
D angerous to defenders.

B edlam to his hairdresser
E nergetic on the pitch
C aptain to England
K icks free kicks like no one else
H appy family man
A way to play in Spain
M arried to Posh Spice.

Gary McGlashan (10)
Greenloaning Primary School, Dunblane

My Family

My auntie Laura,
Is insane,
My uncle Jamie is in lots of pain.

My mum and dad
Are just plain potty.
Gary is a chatterbox
Who talks all day long

And as for me
And as for me
I am perfect
'Cause I am Amy.

Amy McGlashan (7)
Greenloaning Primary School, Dunblane

The Elf's Day Out

There was an elf,
In Santa's house,
Who met a dog,
Who lived on a log.
Then the elf met a frog,
Who ate a log.
They had some fun
And ate a bun,
Yum-yum!
Then he met a clown,
Wearing a crown,
There was a duck,
Who lived in some muck,
But I'm so glad,
That I'm a boy,
Who loves pizza
And is called Lloyd.

Lloyd Rumsby (7)
Greenloaning Primary School, Dunblane

My Pet Dog

My pet dog is a girl,
My pet dog is white,
My pet dog likes to jump,
My pet dog can swim,
My pet dog does all these things,
And she can do more,
More, more, more
And lots more.

Maria Watson (9)
Greenloaning Primary School, Dunblane

Jeepers Creepers

The goblet is hidden
For a Cian to find
Not captain Grimstone, the unkind
The goblet's encrusted
With jewels and diamonds
The blue light haunts
For evil is there
Sending shivers down your spine
You see a death
It could be a friend
You shout and scream
But it never ends
It's damp and dreary you want to get out
Cian is shaken
Captain Grimstone's awakened!

Paula Reid (11)
Hill Primary School, Blairgowrie

Space

Space the invincible void
Never-ending darkness
Meteors hurtling to the ground
Stars thousands of light years away
Astronauts walking on the moon
Silent and forbidding
Mars, the red planet,
Pluto the icy world
Saturn's rings go round and round,
Like an endlessness of space.

Ross Donald (11)
Hill Primary School, Blairgowrie

Hello Dr Frankenstein

Hello Dr Frankenstein,
Did you see the sign?
You must have too much wine,
You were such a fool,
To create a ghoul.

Hello Dr Frankenstein,
You thought it was divine,
You had the time,
You committed crimes,
You used your tools,
To try and rule,
You were cruel,
Deserving of a dual,
Dr Frankenstein.

Jacquelyne MacDonald (11)
Hill Primary School, Blairgowrie

The Glowing Goblet

Cian was left a haunted house,
And Jo was left money,
But Glenderry was not just a house,
It was cursed and full of mystery.

Candles flicker and sometimes go out,
And then there's a foul stench,
Then Captain Grinstone is about,
Looking for the glowing goblet.

There is no sunlight or birds that sing,
It is locked in darkness forever,
Unless they find the Glenderry,
And end this misery!

Lynn Harper (11)
Hill Primary School, Blairgowrie

Dr Frankenstein

Dr Frankenstein,
Who dined on crime,
Made a ghoul,
At six foot nine.
Took the bits, pieces and parts,
And even took emotional hearts.
Put them together,
With a sewing machine,
And then had a break,
And ate scones and cream.
The lightning crashed
And the thunder went *boom*
Good sweet Mike
He's left the room!
The monster roamed
For hours on end,
What's been undone,
He has to mend.
To stop the monsters reappearing
So he did,
And now the doctor is not sneering.

Robyn Taylor (11)
Hill Primary School, Blairgowrie

Sensational Space

Space, the unknown invincible force,
Light years to the nearest star,
The sun like a huge fireball,
Sensational sights of meteorites,
The Milky Way is never-ending,
A multitude of stars surround us,
Space, the unknown invincible force.

Emma Oudney (11)
Hill Primary School, Blairgowrie

The Dangerous Frankenstein

The monstrous Frankenstein,
Committed a crime,
Not only did bad,
But had feelings inside.

The monster of Frankenstein,
Was made up of slime,
With other parts of people,
Including a spine.

The terrifying Frankenstein,
Had an inventor's brain,
Which drove the monster finally insane!

The monster of Frankenstein,
Made up his mind,
And realised, he was
A terrible man inside.

The monster knew he was heading
For the wrong line,
So he killed Dr Frankenstein,
And no longer committed crime!

Laura Gibas (11)
Hill Primary School, Blairgowrie

Mysterious Space

Space, a strange, mysterious blackness
That never ends and the gravity is gone
Sparkling stars all around,
Are sometimes lost and never found
Natural happenings every place, immense impact
Far from home
Meteors hurtling from star to star
Earth to Mars takes time but Mars to Pluto takes
Light years
Space a strange, mysterious place.

Caitlin Duffy (11)
Hill Primary School, Blairgowrie

A Mathematical Poem

About the body,
Everybody has two eyes
And one nose
This everyone knows
Two ears
So we can hear
One mouth to talk
And two legs to walk
Five fingers on each hand
And two feet to walk on land
We have ten toes
And hair that flows
Two arms and a chest
That's where we wear our vest,
But we all have one body
If not, look like something
Out of a comedy.

Alicia Beveridge (11)
Hill Primary School, Blairgowrie

Tom Tiddler

If you go in
The dark, dark forest
You will find a chest,
Of gold and it will be very cold,
Tom Tiddler's long beard,
Will keep you warm,
In the midst of the thunderstorm,
Going through the forest,
You better watch out,
For the great big hand,
Might give you a fright,
The gold will be Tom Tiddler's
In the dark, dark night.

Kevin Robb (11)
Hill Primary School, Blairgowrie

What Did You Do At School Today?

'What did you learn at school today,
Dear little girl of mine?
What did you learn at school today
Dear little girl of mine?'
'I learnt that bullying makes you frantic
I learnt that the Titanic sunk in the Atlantic,
That's what I learnt at school today,
That's what I learnt at school today.'

'What did you learn at school today
Dear little girl of mine?
What did you learn at school today
Dear little girl of mine?'
'I learnt that trees have names
Instead of leaves,
I learnt that Tom Tiddler
Wasn't a fiddler,
That's what I learnt at school today,
That's what I learnt at school today.'

Rachael Lipp (11)
Hill Primary School, Blairgowrie

Space

Space full of microscopic wonders,
Stars implode, meteors explode,
Many suns and universes,
The future is so big and the past is small,
Space probes investigating unanswered mysterious,
Planets are so far away you can't see them in the day.

Holly Seager (11)
Hill Primary School, Blairgowrie

Dr Frankenstein

Every time Dr Frankenstein
Began to mix and match,
Something fine came out of slime
And grew and grew, he was so cruel!
This ghastly ghoul began to pull
With enough power to rule
Deadly disasters began to strike
Night after night with terror and fright.
This monster killed with will of being
So powerful that it got a feeling,
Of poor men squealing.
This ghoul began to *stop*
And be sad about all the power he had
He said, 'Dr Frankenstein your life is now mine!'

Fiona Ritchie (11)
Hill Primary School, Blairgowrie

The Invention

Dr Frankenstein created a ghoul,
To do this he used more than one tool,
He sawed, he chopped and he cut things fine,
A heart, a leg, an arm and a spine,
By murdering people he collected these things,
Legs from dancers and hands from kings,
He put things together, he stuck and he made,
And dressed him in a waistcoat, colour of jade,
He stared at the creature eating crisps
Which were chive,
And then began shouting it's alive, it's alive.

Harley McIntyre (11)
Hill Primary School, Blairgowrie

The Body

From top to bottom,
From left to right,
No matter what you say,
We are all very strange.
We all have one or maybe two voices,
We all have thousands of thoughts,
So no matter what you say,
We are all very strange,
We all have two eyes,
But we all have one mouth,
No matter what you say,
We are all very strange,
Both our hands have fifty bones,
That surely is strange,
We all have ten toes,
That wriggle and can be tickled,
So if you're not convinced,
I suggest you get a new doctor called Vince.

Luke Grant (11)
Hill Primary School, Blairgowrie

Space

Space, endless darkness
Meteors hurtling far and
Near beyond the reach of
Telescopes. Stars imploding
Dying, gravity holding stars
In place. Great supernova in
Stillness, stars identical to the
Naked eye, space, infinite wonder.

John Ellis (11)
Hill Primary School, Blairgowrie

What Did You Learn At School Today?

'What did you learn at school today
Dear little girl of mine?'
'I learnt about space
And its gravity
I learnt about my family tree
And how it goes on for centuries,
This is what I learnt at school today.'

'What did you learn at school today?
What did you learn at school today
Dear little girl of mine?'
'I learnt about bullying
And how it can hurt
I learnt about Tom Tiddler
And how he is a riddler
I learnt about Victoria
And how she had nine kids
And I know how to kick a ball,
That's why I play football,
That's what I learnt at school today,
That's what I learnt at school today.'

Zoe McLaren (11)
Hill Primary School, Blairgowrie

The Ghastly Goblet

The curse was all around the house,
It followed you everywhere,
It was left to young Cian, how did not even care,
He just said, 'It's not fair!'
When Mrs Barry told him of the mystery
He thought she was loppy, like me
But Cian went along with this and kept
On searching for the ghastly goblet.

Daniel Anderson (11)
Hill Primary School, Blairgowrie

The Divine Frankenstein

Dr Frankenstein was so divine,
One day he watched Dr Jekyll and Hyde,
In his little science lab inside,
Frankenstein thought,
I could make a monster.

Frankenstein's monster would
Surely be the worst,
I suppose it would be the first,
The doctor made a terrifying ghoul,
Who would never go to school,
And would always win a duel.

The monster had a third spine,
At the age of twenty-nine,
But the cruel doctor gave him a heart,
Which gave him feelings,
And he didn't kill anymore human beings,
Instead he put a stop
And killed the doc.

Lee Irvine (11)
Hill Primary School, Blairgowrie

Dr Frankenstein

Dr Frankenstein had some wine
And committed a crime
For being a cruel fool
Using lots of tools
And breaking rules
We had a lot of time
In his mind
I hope this is a good rhyme
For Dr Frankenstein,
He kept his cool
Until now as he created the ghoul.

John Cockburn (11)
Hill Primary School, Blairgowrie

Smoking

Smoking isn't cool,
You're putting horrible drugs into your body,
And into other's people's too,
You take three types of chemicals in if you smoke -
Nicotine, carbon monoxide and tar,
Which stick to everything before
It goes down into your lungs and
Makes you unhealthy and unwell,
Smoking makes you all smelly and wrinkly and
Your lungs all black and blue,
You're passing all the smoke on to your friends and
People around you,
So you're lucky if they want to hang around with you,
You're spending lots of money on bad health,
Cigarettes could cost you your *life!*
Smoking will harm you!
Don't start!

Shauni Robinson (10)
Hill Primary School, Blairgowrie

The Goblet

Cian O'Horgan's name has been in their
Family for generations.
In an old and spooky mansion
Is a curse to be banished,
Mrs Barry hurt her leg,
Went to hospital on a bed,
Jo and Cian left alone to
Banish the curse on their home.
Mum won't be back until tomorrow
Because of the flood.
So in the house Cian and Jo
Stuck in the house, scared to go.
Captain Grimstone haunting the house
Flinging chairs all about.

Kris Nesbitt (11)
Hill Primary School, Blairgowrie

Stop Smoking

Don't you smoke or you will choke
You better stop or you will pop
Yellow fingers, stinking hair
I bet these are things you cannot bear.

If you smoke you're a fool
If you smoke you're not cool
Soon your voice will start croaking
Everyone around you will feel like boking.

Smoking costs a lot of money
So smoking really is not funny
Passive smoking can cause disease
I would not like that if you please!
Stop smoking.

Ryan Lynn (11)
Hill Primary School, Blairgowrie

The Curse Of Glenderry House

Glenderry House cursed evermore,
Ghosts and ghouls scream and roar,
Captain Grimstone cursed for eternity,
Haunting the O'Horgan family.

No plants grow and no birds sing,
And in the house objects fling.
There is a terrible stench in the hall,
Where Mrs Barry had her fall.
They used some candles out of a box,
After they had seen the captain, they stopped.
The goblet hidden nice and neat,
Nobody will find it especially Fred or Pete.

Ryan Feaks (11)
Hill Primary School, Blairgowrie

Grimstone's Goblet

Cian to Cian,
This curse does go,
Where the goblet is,
Cian does not know!

The light in the shrubs,
Was how it started,
Off to the hospital,
Mrs Barry was carted!

On their own,
Cian and Jo must find,
The goblet,
Cian is going out of his mind!

They must have used dozens of candles,
Cian is angry,
The blue light is as bad as 100 vandals.

Mum is stuck 20 miles away
She will be back the very next day,
But what if she's too late?
Why couldn't Cian just be called Kate?

So in the house,
The children are stuck,
Jo and Cian don't have much luck!

But maybe they'll find the goblet,
But maybe they won't!
We'll have to wait,
What if Mum's too late?

Robyn Smith (11)
Hill Primary School, Blairgowrie

Smokin' Ain't Cool

Smokin' ain't cool,
It don't make the kiddies drool,
If you smoke, you must be a fool.

It poisons your lungs and your heart,
All to make you look so smart,
But it doesn't!

Smokin' ain't cool,
It don't make the kiddies drool,
If you smoke, you must be a fool.

It doesn't calm you down,
Or take away stress
All it does is leave you in a mess,
Don't do it!

Smokin' ain't cool,
It don't make the kiddies drool
If you smoke, you must be a fool.

Your teeth go black,
Like soot in a sack.

Smokin' ain't cool,
It don't make the kiddies drool,
If you smoke, you must be a fool,
Don't smoke!

Emily Cuthill (11)
Hill Primary School, Blairgowrie

Smoking

When you breathe in cigarette smoke,
It's horrible and smelly,
Within a couple of days,
Your fingertips go yelly.

Children as young as ten smoke,
Day after day,
By the age of sixteen,
They've thrown their life away.

Cigarettes are a number one killer,
They push your friends away,
Once you've smoked a couple,
The habit's there to stay.

Nicotine makes your heart beat faster,
And leaves you out of breath,
I don't know how to say this,
But it ends up in your death!

Kathryn Forsyth (11)
Hill Primary School, Blairgowrie

Space Poem

What an amazing
Spectrum glowing from
The stars and planets!
Unvisited universes
That nobody can
Even imagine or
Explore. Stars
Exploding and imploding.
The return of the
Halley's Comet every 76 years.
What an amazing spectrum.

Roy Edgar (11)
Hill Primary School, Blairgowrie

Smoking

Smoking ain't cool
You will just be a fool
It gives you lung cancer
Or heart disease
So please don't smoke.

You will get yellow fingers
You will get smelly hair
It causes cancer
It is not healthy
So please don't smoke.

When you're at the age
Make the right choice
Don't smoke please
Be healthy
Don't smoke.

Why chuck your life away?
You can play every single day
You will never regret it
Stay away from fags.

So take my advice
Live your life nice.

Hayley Douglas (11)
Hill Primary School, Blairgowrie

Smoking Kills

Smoking is a waste of your life
Cigarettes pollute you with
Nicotine and tar and poisonous gases,
The effects are bad, yellow fingers,
Smelly hair, lack of breath,
Death!

Grant Kellie (11)
Hill Primary School, Blairgowrie

Smoking

If you smoke five packs of cigarettes a day,
Then you are going right out of your way
To make yourself ill and fill your lungs with tar
Soon you won't be able to walk very far.

Smoking makes your breath stinky
Your teeth become stained and your skin
Goes all wrinkly,
The warnings on the packets and the adverts on TV,
I am telling you to stop why can't you just see?

Your cigarette smoke can make children ill,
Passive smoking it's called and it really can kill,
Haven't you see the advert when the smoke
Goes round the baby's neck?
The next thing is it's in hospital, oh heck!

So what I am saying is smoking's not smart,
It's really hard to stop so it's better not to start!

Beth McIntyre (11)
Hill Primary School, Blairgowrie

Don't Smoke

Don't smoke it's bad for you,
Don't smoke nicotine, cos you'll stink poo-woo!
If you smoke get out of here,
Now we know that there is smoke near.

When you're driving in your car
And both your lungs are full of tar
That will cause a lot of damage
So stop your smoking and try to manage.

Don't smoke, it doesn't make you smart
It makes you stink and is bad for your heart.

So don't smoke - it's not a joke!

Lori Cabena (11)
Hill Primary School, Blairgowrie

Around The World

Around the world
Round and round
The spinning world
The moon goes flying
I'm sure it's winning
The race for spinning.

Around the world
The spinning world
The birds and bees
In the air go flying
And shiny fish
Swim round their dish.

Around the world
The clouds go flying
In the big blue sky
Of the spinning world
That spins in a race
In outer space.

Finlay Page (11)
Hill Primary School, Blairgowrie

Smoking

Smoking! When you start,
It goes straight to your heart,
You may think it's fun
But what about your lungs?

You want to be the best footballer in all the land
But have you ever seen a footballer
With a fag in his hand?

When that first cigarette touches your lips
You're just throwing yourself into a bottomless pit.

You could live till you're 94,
But if you smoke, you'll end up dead on the floor!

Rosie Wilson (11)
Hill Primary School, Blairgowrie

Ten Centimetres Tall

I'm ten centimetres tall
I'm very, very small
I'm struggling through a jungle
Of grass and muddy soil
Huge, green-coloured stems
Of cup sized daisies
Weave around me
Like a tangle of spaghetti.
A large green croaking monster
Of a bulging-eyed frog
Stares out of the tall green-bladed grass
Then jumps around like a rabbit
Leaving footprints in the mud
The size of lakes.
In the distance a large trail
Of marching soldiered ants
With deep brown shiny skin
And big kangaroo feet
March towards me
The ground rumbles
Like an earthquake
And high on a mole mountain
A slimy snaky worm slithers down
Leaving a trail
As long as a ruler.
Yes I'm really, very small
Only ten centimetres tall
And I'm struggling through a jungle
Of grass and muddy soil.

Calley Leith (11)
Hill Primary School, Blairgowrie

Don't Smoke

Don't smoke
It's not good for you
Your fingers turn yellow
And your hair stinks too,
You'll find it hard to breathe,
If you start to smoke,
So in my opinion
You're really being a dope.

On big fat fags you'll
Spend all your money
And won't have enough left
To go on holiday
Somewhere sunny.

If you start smoking you'll
Just get worse and worse,
You'll be addicted and
Keep going until your lungs burst.

So what I'm trying to say
If someone offers
You a cigarette
Is just say *no* and
Send them on their way.

Hayley Grant (11)
Hill Primary School, Blairgowrie

Around The World

Every day
Around the world
Invisible messages
Fly to phones
With funny ring tones
One day
Around the world
People could travel
On giant birds
Or UFOs
Or unseen
Invisible travelling
Mysteries unravelling
So maybe some day
Around the world
Even pigs might fly!

Jamie Stewart (11)
Hill Primary School, Blairgowrie

Around The World

If the world is round, in fact a sphere
Then how come we are all still here?
If the world is spinning round and round
What is keeping everything on the ground?
If around the world there's climates and seasons
What's it all for? There must be a reason.
As I travel around the world from place to place
Why don't I fall off into outer space?
If around the world there's atmosphere
How come I can't see it from here?
And why does the sky seem to go on and on?
I'll have to stop there. Where has the time gone?

Jade Webster (11)
Hill Primary School, Blairgowrie

Smoking

Smoking ain't cool
Smoking ain't smart
It's bad for your lungs
And even worse for your heart.
If you start smoking now
It may seem like a thrill
But you won't live long
Because the nicotine will kill
People think smoking
Helps them cope with stress
They are actually wrong
It leaves a dirty, smelly mess
It makes your fingers stained
And your heart beat faster
It leaves you out of breath
And you can't run any faster.

Storm Andrews (11)
Hill Primary School, Blairgowrie

Smoking Don't Do It!

If you smoke you
Cough and choke
And your teeth will stain
You'll be left with heart pain
When the tar sticks to your lungs
You will be damaged for years to come
If you smoke and think you're cool
In fact you're actually a fool
You won't think it's very funny
When smoking takes away all your money
The chemicals will ruin your life
And you'll find it hard to get a wife.

Matthew Parker (11)
Hill Primary School, Blairgowrie

Don't Smoke!

Don't smoke
It'll make
You croak.
It'll make
You smell
And you'll
Feel unwell.
It'll make
You ill
It can even
Kill!
Smoking's not
Fun. It's really
Dumb!
Don't smoke
It doesn't make
You wealthy.
It makes you
Unhealthy!

Zoe Irvine (12)
Hill Primary School, Blairgowrie

Around The World

Around the world
There is a blanket
Of invisible air
The ozone layer
It helps protect us
But it is getting thin
The sun's rays are shining through
Giving us light
And too much heat
And we can see through the holes
Right into space
Where the moon orbits the Earth
Controlling our tides
Giving us day and night
Reflecting more sunlight
Around the world.

Georgia Bell (11)
Hill Primary School, Blairgowrie

Hallowe'en

H allowe'en is horrible and mean,

A t night witches fly out and give you a fright,

L egs of spiders, hairy and black, scurry up the wall,

L ike black cats on witches' hats,

O ne ghastly ghost appears through the old door,

W ild demons come out of the walls and scare the socks off you,

E veryone joins the horrible Hallowe'en party,

E ight legged freaks appear from thin air,

N ever fear your mummy's here, the end of Hallowe'en is near!

John Thomson (11)
Invergarry Primary School, Invergarry

Autumn

Autumn has come and the ground is a bed of leaves,
The trees are bare but a day will come when new leaves sprout,
Wind is strong and whirls the leaves around the town,
Children come out and play on this autumn day,
Autumn is a colourful work of art,
This season will soon be blanked out with winter.

Kelly MacDiarmid (10)
Invergarry Primary School, Invergarry

Winter

As the snow covers the ground with a white velvet blanket,
Children sledge down the snow covered hills,
People wrap up in scarves, gloves and big woolly hats,
While others sit down at the fire and warm away the winter chills,
Cars go skidding on the ice
And the roads block up with snow,
And that's what makes winter nice.

Laura Stewart (10)
Invergarry Primary School, Invergarry

Sadness

Sadness is the colour of a blue tear dripping down my face,
It tastes like cold water slipping down my throat,
It smells like a cold, damp corner on a misty day,
It looks like a little child crying for his mum,
It sounds like rain dripping on the ground,
It feels like burying your own pet when it's just died.

Kirsty Mackenzie (9)
Invergarry Primary School, Invergarry

Sadness

Sadness is the colour of grey clouds covering
Up the lovely, clear, blue sky,
It tastes like cold porridge on a winter's day,
It smells like smoke coming out of a chimney,
It looks like my mum's face at my gran's funeral,
It sounds like me crying for my uncle Iain,
It feels like you're all alone.

Alysha Henderson (9)
Invergarry Primary School, Invergarry

Happiness

Happiness is blue like the morning sky,
It tastes like a hot Mars bar melting in my mouth,
It smells of freshly cut roses on a hot summer's day,
It looks like a big, colourful rainbow at the
End of a drizzly afternoon,
It sounds like people joyfully splashing in the pool,
It feels like being over the moon!

Rebecca Martin (10)
Invergarry Primary School, Invergarry

Happiness

Happiness is like fresh grass on a summer's morning,
It tastes like juicy, sweet, fresh orange,
It smells like fresh air,
It looks like people splashing in the water,
It sounds like birds singing softly,
It feels like getting into a fresh bed.

Robert Shepherd (10)
Invergarry Primary School, Invergarry

Happiness

Happiness is blue like the morning sky,
It tastes like hot apple pie,
It smells like newly cut grass,
It looks like Mum on a night out,
It sounds like the wind howling through the trees,
It feels like the soft, silky leather of my
Gloves on my hands.

Matthew MacCallum (9)
Invergarry Primary School, Invergarry

Comet

His eyes are as black as coal,
His teeth are as sharp as broken glass,
His fur is as soft as velvet,
His face is as small as a 10p coin,
His tail is like a snake zigzagging
Along the ground,
Who is he? He's my pet gerbil!

Daniel Channon (11)
Kilry Primary School, Blairgowrie

Reading

Why do I like Harry Potter books?
I like them because they are magical,
Like running through a wall to Platform 9¾s,
I like them because they are exciting,
Like the night before Christmas Day,
I like them because they get longer and longer,
Like The Lord of the Rings,
I like them because they are funny,
Like when Hagrid comes bursting through the door.

Grant Walker (12)
Kilry Primary School, Blairgowrie

My Pet Dogs

Why do I like dogs so much?
Corrie is as brave as a soldier at war,
Heather is as fast as a rock falling off a cliff,
Corrie is as active as an athlete winning the
Olympic Games,
Heather is as friendly as someone making
A bully a friend,
Corrie is as protective as the military and the queen.
This is why!

Cameron Martindale (10)
Kilry Primary School, Blairgowrie

Trapped

I felt rumbling underneath my feet,
I saw gravel thumping on the ground,
I was very frightened because I felt that
I was going to die,
I tasted the dust from the ground
Going into my face,
I thought that I would never be found,
I was excited when I heard the rescue men and dogs.

Steven Walker (10)
Kilry Primary School, Blairgowrie

My Best Friend

She is as smart as two adult brains stuck together!
She is as kind as a cute little kitten curling up on
My lap with its claws tucked in!
She is as dainty as a fairy skipping on a pansy leaf,
Her hair is as black as freshly polished school shoes,
Her smile reminds me of a Cheshire cat,
Who wouldn't like my best friend?

Catriona Ferguson (9)
Kilry Primary School, Blairgowrie

Trapped

I could see nothing but shadows and broken rock,
I could hear nothing but broken rocks being moved around,
I could feel my skin which felt very hard and really scaly,
I could taste nothing but grit and dust in my mouth,
I could smell nothing but mould and dust floating about,
I felt very uncomfortable and a bit panicky.

I could see nothing except the blue sky above me,
I could only hear men asking me how I felt,
I could feel a drop of cool and fresh spring water on my lips,
I could taste it wash through my mouth,
I could smell the petrol of the fire engine,
I felt very happy to be alive and thought it was a miracle.

Gabriella Hall (11)
Kilry Primary School, Blairgowrie

Walter's Wave

I feel fuzzy and warm and cosy inside
As he passes by on his quad.

When I am feeling down, it brightens my day
So I am cheerful and happy.

I smile to myself when he has gone by like
A Cheshire cat with a big grin on her face.

His very friendly personality shines through and
Brightens up the whole district.

He sticks his hand into the air like he is
Reaching for the sky.

Walter a funny, friendly man.

Rosalyn Hall (10)
Kilry Primary School, Blairgowrie

My New Brother

The expression on his face when he is
Sleeping is like he has eaten the most
Disgusting thing in the world.

His tiny, little fingers grab you stronger than a crocodile.

His cry is as loud as thunder up in the sky.

His hair is softer than cats and dogs fur put together.

He is as small as a newborn cheetah.

When he is quiet, he reminds me of two minutes silence.
That's my new brother,
Finlay!

Marcus De Vale (9)
Kilry Primary School, Blairgowrie

Sammy My Rabbit

His fur is as soft as a woolly jumper, and when
I cuddle him I feel happy!
His ears are as big, as a big soft banana,
His bobby tail is as round as a ball of wool
And when he thumps his tail, I know he's happy,
His pure black and white colour is as pure
As pure oil and snow,
When he gets his carrots, I can smell and taste them,
When he is good, he is as good as a lamb,
But when he isn't, he's a lion trying to scratch me!

This is why I love him.

Emma Bryce (9)
Kilry Primary School, Blairgowrie

You And I

We are different
Each of us look different

A pair of twins are nearly the same
Read different
Each of the people are different but twins are sort of the same

Different people make the world fun
If you and I were the same it would be boring
Fun world fun people and you and I different
Find people easy
Each and every own are different
Reads different authors
Each of us people
Nobody is the same
Tell everybody.

Ross MacLeod (10)
Marybank Primary School, Urray

Rainforests

R ight round the forest covered in animals and
A ll the apes are playing in their habitats.
 I ndians are hunting
N ight is falling
F rogs are leaping to go home.
O n the ground the moonlight shines
R ight through the night
E verything is loud and most of the animals are sleeping
S nakes are slithering.
T oday is a day for life.

Ryan MacMillan (10)
Marybank Primary School, Urray

Panto Days

P ositions to be learnt
A ctors better than me
N ever-ending fun
T oday and every other day
O n stage and off stage
M istakes being made and sorted
I tchy costumes and make-up to be worn
M onday to Sunday all day long
E verlasting fun.

Fiona Fraser (11)
Marybank Primary School, Urray

Fire Fly

One dark night,
A band of fireflies came to light.
Away they flew,
Over to you,
And lit up your face in the night.
You jumped, you screamed,
You got a fright,
Away they flew in a cloud of light.

Blabheinn Mackintosh (10)
Marybank Primary School, Urray

Elephants

Elephants laugh, elephants cry.
Every elephant eats pie!
Elephants sing, elephants hum,
All day long they sit on their bum!
Elephants are heavy, elephants are light.
Elephants' clothes are always so bright!

Helen Matheson (10)
Marybank Primary School, Urray

Rainforests

R ain thundering down.
A ll is safely sleeping, sleeping at night,
I n the morning everything is flooded,
N othing seems to stir.
F orests, forests all I see,
O pening my eyes wide.
R oaring waterfalls,
E verything is still,
S mells are all around,
T hrough the air and on the ground.

Brian Finlayson (11)
Marybank Primary School, Urray

The Tide

The tide brings fins
Sharp, blunt, curved fins
The tide pulls them back again.
The tide brings seaweed
Sharp, dry, short seaweed.

The tide brings shells
Long, small, curved shells
The tide pulls them back again.
The tide brings rocks
Hard, round, small rocks.

The tide brings fish
Smelly, dirty, long, small fish
The tide pulls them back again.
The tide brings rubbish
Smelly, dirty, stinky rubbish.

James Smith (9)
Moncreiffe Primary School, Perth

The Tide

The tide brings shells
Big, long, patterned shells
The bubbly tide pulls them back again.

The tide brings jellyfish
Wobbly, slimy, clear jellyfish.
The crashing tide pulls them back again.

The tide brings rocks
Rough, smooth, jaggy rocks.
The moving tide pulls them back again.

The tide brings seaweed
Straggly, smelly, salty seaweed.
The freezing tide pulls them back again.

The tide brings fish
Smelly, rotten, old fish.
The clear tide pulls them back again.

Kirsteen MacSween (9)
Moncreiffe Primary School, Perth

We Like

We like to squeeze our apples
We like to squeeze our bananas
And when we are feeling sad
We like to squeeze our nannas.

We like to run round our gardens
We like to walk the streets
And when we are really bored
We like to sit and eat.

Laura McLean (9)
Moncreiffe Primary School, Perth

The Tide

The tide brings shells
Small, smooth, clean, cool shells
The tide pulls them back again.

The tide brings bottles
Transparent, clear, long bottles
The strong tide pulls them back again.

The cold tide brings crabs
Dead, hard, rough crabs
The rough tide pulls them back again.

The rising tide brings rubbish
Light, blowy, empty rubbish
The wavy tide pulls them back again.

Sam Edward (9)
Moncreiffe Primary School, Perth

The Tide

The rough tide brings drift wood
Old jaggy, soggy drift wood.
The tide pulls it back again.

The rough tide brings seaweed
Straggly, smelly, salty seaweed.
The tide pulls it back again.

The rough tide brings crabs
Moving, snappy, dragging crabs.
The tide pulls them back again.

The rough tide brings shingles
Small, sharp, brown shingles.
The tide pulls them back again.

Jodie McBeath (9)
Moncreiffe Primary School, Perth

The Tide

The tide brings shells
Smooth, hard, sharp, spiral shells.
The rough tide pulls them back again.
The tide brings periwinkles
Robust, dull, grey, black periwinkles.
The strong tide pulls them back again.
The tide brings starfish
Pointy, spotty, orange starfish.
The wavy tide pulls them back again.
The tide brings limpets
Pale, grey, rough limpets.
The low tide pulls them back again.
The tide brings sponges
Rotten, smelly, squidgy sponges.
The smelly tide pulls them back again.

Deanna Green (9)
Moncreiffe Primary School, Perth

The Tide

The tide brings shells,
Rough, jaggy shells.
The tide pulls them back again.
The tide brings seaweed.
The tide pulls it back again.
The tide brings rocks,
Hard, spiky rocks.
The tide takes them back again.
The tide brings crabs,
Nippy red crabs.
The tide takes them back again.

Dean MacFarlane (9)
Moncreiffe Primary School, Perth

The Tide

The tide brings seaweed,
Long, green seaweed,
The strong tide pulls it back again.

The tide brings shells,
Big shells and small shells,
The freezing tide pulls them back again.

The tide brings rocks,
Sharp rocks, smooth rocks,
The blue tide pulls them back again.

The tide brings fish,
Old rotten fish,
The clear tide brings them back again.

Sarah Watt (10)
Moncreiffe Primary School, Perth

The Tide

The tide brings shells
Long, small, curved, ribbed shells
The tide pulls them back again.

The low tide brings seaweed
Straggly, salty, smelly, wet seaweed
The low tide pulls it back again.

The high tide brings rocks
Hard, small, smooth, rough rocks
The high tide pulls them back again.

Kayleigh Burnside (9)
Moncreiffe Primary School, Perth

The Tide

The tide brings shells
Smooth, hard, sharp, spiral shell
The rough tide brings them back again.

The tide brings periwinkles sometimes
Smooth, sometimes rough and all sorts of coloured periwinkles
The tide brings them back again.

The tide bring limpets
Rough, bumpy and smooth inside limpets
The tide brings them back again.

The tide brings razor shells
Sharp, long or short razor shells
The tide brings them back again.

Sophie Claire Moyes (9)
Moncreiffe Primary School, Perth

The Tide

The tide brings shells
Rough, jaggy shells
The tide pulls them back again
The low tide brings seaweed
Smooth, gungy seaweed
The tide pulls it back again
The high tide brings rocks
Rough, spiky rocks
The high tide pulls them back again.

Julie Ann MacNeil (8)
Moncreiffe Primary School, Perth

The Tide

The tide brings shells
Sharp, smooth, rough, long shells
The trickling tide brings them back again
The tide brings seaweed
Slimy, soggy, smelly, gooey seaweed
The foaming tide brings them back again
The tide brings bones
Skinny, pointy, curvy, fat bones
The sprinkling tide brings them back again
The tide brings pebbles
Smooth, shiny, soft, rough pebbles
The splashing tide brings them back again.

Abigail Williams (9)
Moncreiffe Primary School, Perth

The Tide

The tide brings shells
Big, long, patterned shells
The bubbly tide pulls them back again

The tide brings jellyfish
Wobbly, clear, slimy jellyfish
The crashing tide pulls them back again

The tide brings rocks
Rough smooth jagged rocks
The moving tide pulls them back again.

Linzi Martin (9)
Moncreiffe Primary School, Perth

Winter Song

Cheerful children snowballs throw,
Children's little fingers glow,
Fingers glow,
 Fingers glow,
  Fingers glow.

Lauren MacKenzie (9)
Mount Pleasant Primary School, Thurso

Winter Song

Winter winds bring the snow,
Crunching, crackling, snowballs go,
Snowballs go,
 Snowballs go,
  Snowballs go.

Michaela Cameron (9)
Mount Pleasant Primary School, Thurso

Winter Song

No flowers are peeping from below
and somehow the river has no flow,
has no flow,
 has no flow,
  has no flow.

Caitlin Souter (9)
Mount Pleasant Primary School, Thurso

Winter Song

The snow has come, the cars can't go,
but here comes the snow plough, he'll make the traffic flow,
traffic flow,
    traffic flow,
        traffic flow.

Kasey MacLean (10)
Mount Pleasant Primary School, Thurso

Winter Song

Time to go in, but we all know,
we'll be back tomorrow though,
tomorrow
    though,
        tomorrow
            though,
                tomorrow
                    though.

Ryan Swanson (9)
Mount Pleasant Primary School, Thurso

Winter Song

Will the snow last? I don't think so,
Overnight it might go,
It might go,
    It might go,
        It might go.

Steven Firth (9)
Mount Pleasant Primary School, Thurso

Winter Song

The river's frozen, the boats won't row,
but under the water, the fish still flow,
the fish still flow,
    the fish still flow,
        the fish still flow.

Jordan Jones (9)
Mount Pleasant Primary School, Thurso

Winter Song

Winds blow high, winds blow low,
Howling through the closed window,
Closed window,
    Closed window,
        Closed window.

Tammy Rendall (9)
Mount Pleasant Primary School, Thurso

Winter Song

The plants below are sleeping in the snow,
Here comes the snow with its glittery glow,
Glittery glow,
    Glittery glow,
        Glittery glow.

Rachael Canavan (9)
Mount Pleasant Primary School, Thurso

Winter Song

We build a snowman in the snow
and two days later he will go
he will go
he will go
he will go.

Shannon Swanson (8)
Mount Pleasant Primary School, Thurso

Winter Song

I'm skating on the ice - very, very slow,
but still I've been able to break my toe,
break my toe,
break my toe,
break my toe.

Liam Elder (9)
Mount Pleasant Primary School, Thurso

Winter Song

The ice is here, it's slippery oh no!
I'll have to be careful in case I fall, though,
In case I fall though,
In case I fall though,
In case I fall though.

Stacey Waters (9)
Mount Pleasant Primary School, Thurso

Winter Song

Snowflakes fall gently on the window,
Will there be school tomorrow?
School tomorrow?
    School tomorrow?
        School tomorrow?

Kerr MacKay, Chloe Elder & Ross MacKay (9)
Mount Pleasant Primary School, Thurso

Winter Song

The planes won't go, not even at Heathrow,
Down comes the snow, we are snowed in, 'Oh no!'
Snowed in, 'Oh no!'
    Snowed in, 'Oh no!'
        Snowed in, 'Oh no!'

Danny Gunn (10), Jenni Hinds & Liam Begg (9)
Mount Pleasant Primary School, Thurso

Winter Song

The snow will come, the river won't flow
The snowman turns round and says, 'Hello,'
Says, 'Hello,'
    Says, 'Hello,'
        Says, 'Hello.'

Laura McPhee (9)
Mount Pleasant Primary School, Thurso

The Sky

The sky is like the ocean, never quite the same.
Where its candyfloss clouds lay.
The birds fly and soar against the piercing sun.
While underneath them the sea calmly drums.
But if something goes wrong the hail comes on.
Coming, not like soft snow falling on the ground.
It pelts on the windows and blows away the birds.
It hits against my forehead and makes me frown.

Susan Mair (11)
Mount Pleasant Primary School, Thurso

Winter Song

The snow is falling on the shiny window,
In the garden the cheery snowman shouts, 'Hello hello!'
'Hello hello!'
   'Hello hello!'
      'Hello hello!'

Ellie MacKrell (9)
Mount Pleasant Primary School, Thurso

Winter Song

We make a snowball in the snow,
And then we throw it and watch it go,
Watch it go,
   Watch it go,
      Watch it go.

Amy Munro (9)
Mount Pleasant Primary School, Thurso

Sooo Petrifying

They came with a sword
A spear and a shield
They came in their long ship to get there,
They shot us and stabbed us
And we trembled with fear,
We were shocked by what came here!
Those horrifying men destroyed and burned,
But now we were certain that they had returned
They shot my mother
And stabbed my brother
They loved to murder
They came with thunder
Sooo petrifying!
They stole all our jewellery
Our gold and our silver
They took all our plates and cups too,
Completely demolished our village
I think you should be happy
They didn't try and get you!
They murdered my father
Killed the monks with a dagger
And to go even further
They took all the treasure
Just for pleasure . . .
Sooo petrifying
The Vikings!

Melissa J Bremner (8)
New Deer Primary School, Turriff

The Vikings Attack

This terrible attack on Lindisfarne
Blood splattered everywhere
Treasures have been stolen
The buildings have been burned,
And children and parents are crying.

Casey Anderson (8)
New Deer Primary School, Turriff

Astonishing Vikings

Vikings are astonishing gliding through the sea in their longboats.
As they glide through the sea they sing a song with a melody.
Longboats with dragons are so scary that you would jump.
Weapons clatter as the Vikings come closer, ready to fight the
Vikings attack.
They steal from the monastery, that's really bad they steal goblets,
gold and silver too and much, much more.
It is so shocking as the monks just stand as the Vikings kill.
No fighting they do as they are holy people
Venomous things the Vikings do, that is certainly not the life for you.
Petrified the monks stare.
They steal and they kill for pleasure.
The enormous Vikings are so scary that everybody trembles in
their skin.
They kill everybody
With bloodstained swords slippery as they fight.
They go back to their wonderful country with tremendous ffjords and
mountains and lovely scenery.
They go to sleep and when they wake in the morning they are ready to
fight the next day.

Vivienne Jackson (8)
New Deer Primary School, Turriff

Viking Poem

Tangled hair, mystic eyes, red ears and a big broad back.
They attack, they kill, they terrorise, they burn
They steal treasure
And kill monks for pleasure
They have swords with such names as nose picker
They take out eyes with them
And even make people cry with them
They sail on long ships with dragons' heads
You'll be dead if you see that dragon's head.

Morag Brown (8)
New Deer Primary School, Turriff

Here Comes Trouble

Today I heard terror
Today I heard shouting
Today I heard 'Vikings'
Tearing over mountains
Tearing over land
With their feet of thunder
Attacking all the monks as they soared by
People screaming with terror
They sliced off their heads
And left the blood and bodies
Around the town
Pushed people to the sides
And stabbed them
They left in their long ships with shields and dragon's head and tail
Getting to their land
All it takes a week or two, getting to their houses
Getting their supper, washing their clothes
Sorting their weapons
Now these are Vikings of terror.

Jake Earl (8)
New Deer Primary School, Turriff

100 Years Ago

The Vikings *attacked* the monastery
All the monks died
A Viking planned to kill the monks
They prepared for battle
The Vikings came for a battle
Against the monks.
The monks died
All the survivors took the weapons
After the battle.

Nicholas Mickowski (8)
New Deer Primary School, Turriff

The Vikings Return

At Lindisfarne
Vikings killed monks
Burned houses
Attacked the monastery
I was crying
Because my mum and dad were going to die
Until I heard a splatter of blood
I didn't know who it was
Until a Viking came and saw me
I ran away
I saw my den
And when I went into my den
I saw my mum and dad
I gave them a hug
And they said, 'I don't want you to go out there again.'

Tamara Stockdale (8)
New Deer Primary School, Turriff

The Vikings Return

Terrifying Vikings attack
Scary longboats burn
Horrifying swords stab
Shiny treasure stolen
Brilliant mountains shake
Stunning fjords shimmer
Fearsome fire kills
Decorative designs destroyed
Enormous spears stab
Terrific Danish travellers
Skilful monks sob
Many monasteries demolished
Sneaky Norsemen terrorise
Petrified people perished.

Brian Martin (8)
New Deer Primary School, Turriff

Here Are The Vikings!

The Vikings are here,
To steal all the treasure,
The monks are now dead,
And the treasure has been stolen,
By the horrible Vikings.
The Vikings are disgusting, ugly and so horrible.
They are also mean and never let the monks live in peace.
The monastery is burning and guess who it was?
That's right, the Vikings!
The Vikings had lived,
In 793AD,
They were surrounded,
By lots and lots of weapons.
Spears, swords and shields,
Were some of the goodies,
That the Vikings used!
'The monks are going to die!'
Said the Viking god, Thor
With the hammer.
That was hard.
He was very thick
But had big muscles.

Stuart Milne (8)
New Deer Primary School, Turriff

The Vikings

The Vikings raided islands for treasure.
They killed and took people for all pleasure.
The Vikings were horrifying
and they were terrifying.
But the Vikings were also very cunning,
they knew that the monks did not go running.
The Vikings were horrifying
and they were terrifying.

Savannah Copland (8)
New Deer Primary School, Turriff

Viking Poem

Dinna even think of passing by a Viking.
Their teeth are dirty and their food is green.
I wouldna hay that in my hoose.
I wouldna think you like to see a richt bonny Viking.
An one thing else I've got a wife as well.
But I ken all about Vikings.
Guess why?
We're Vikings ourselves!

Sophie Dalgarno (8)
New Deer Primary School, Turriff

Vikings

These terrifying men came to our land
They killed the people who I have known for years
They killed my family as well.
We knew they were bad men right from the start.
These horrible, dirty, smelly men
With tangled beards and food stuck in them.
They were the Vikings.

Natasha Forrest (8)
New Deer Primary School, Turriff

Here Come The Vikings

Vikings are fierce men who kill people.
Vikings are called Norse men.
They are scary people as well.
They can sneak up on you
If you're not in a good hiding place.

Kathleen McDonald (8)
New Deer Primary School, Turriff

The Viking Terror!

The Vikings had steamy faces.
And scary and fierce curly hair.
Vikings with lightning in their bellies.
And dragons with
Bloodstained skin.
Their longboats were terrific.
The Vikings had baggy clothes.
And terrifying weapons.
And terrible and frightening helmets.

Molly Gibson (8)
New Deer Primary School, Turriff

Here Come The Vikings

You hear the thunder,
You hear the crash,
You see the Viking ship
They come sneaking
They come to Lindisfarne,
To attack.

Jacqueline Kindness (8)
New Deer Primary School, Turriff

Vikings

Scary Viking attack
Monks scream out loud
Vikings take some monks to be slaves
And kill some
They take the monks to the boat
And they sail off.

Ryan Norrie (8)
New Deer Primary School, Turriff

Vikings

Vikings were bad the left the people sad.
They were kind of mad.
They killed the lads.

They sailed in a boat across the moat.
They had big red coats.
They cut people's throats.

They stole people's money
Which wasn't very funny.
They killed lots of bunnies
And upset the mummies.

Laura Simpson (9)
New Deer Primary School, Turriff

Here Come The Vikings

The Vikings were sneaky and hairy,
Their swords were slippery and scary.
Their feet clashed like thunder and rain,
They killed the monks and took no blame.
They attacked, they killed, they destroyed, they stabbed.
They made other people die and made some people mad.
Their longboats swished and splashed,
But if they'd fallen out of it it would have made a clash.

Amy Brain (8)
New Deer Primary School, Turriff

A Snowy Day

It is snowing today,
Oh what a time to play.
The frosty snowflakes
Are heading right my way.

I like to have a snowball fight,
Every single day and night.
Do you like snow?
Throwing it to and fro,
Making snowmen and angel shapes,
Having snow wars with your mates,
With snow you have so much to do,
I know you like it because I do too!

Lucy Deakin (10)
Scourie Primary School, Scourie by Lairg

A Rainbow

I like rainbows
Do you?
They are nice and tall and
Sometimes small.
I always dream that if I follow it,
I will find a pot of gold at the bottom of it.
I like how rainbows have different colours
Like red, orange, yellow and blue,
Green and indigo and violet.
I love rainbows.

Jo Fraser (10)
Scourie Primary School, Scourie by Lairg

There Once Were Some Animals

There once was a young cat,
Who liked to wear a hat.
He wore boots on his feet,
And shook hands with the people he'd meet.

There once was an old horse,
Who ate apples of course.
She would have a nap
And look at a map
To go right around the field.

There once was a dog,
Owned by a hog.
He ran away,
Every day,
But came home to play.

Sophie Deakin (8)
Scourie Primary School, Scourie by Lairg

Football

Football is my life,
I play it every day,
I eat it, sleep it and dream it twice,
Every single day.

Football is my life,
I want to be a pro,
But before I do I'd like,
To eat it, sleep it and dream it,
Just once more.

Eilidh MacFarlane (10)
Scourie Primary School, Scourie by Lairg

Puppies

P uppies playful all the time.
U nder the sun for a run.
P addling in the water
P aws are really wet.
I t is great having a puppy.
E nd of the day go to sleep.
S leep little puppy, it's time to sleep.

Mathew Hathaway (8)
Scourie Primary School, Scourie by Lairg

Invisible Mike

Mike is my friend,
He likes to pretend,
That he's at the moon,
And he'll be back soon.

Mike is my pal,
I read him Roald Dahl,
He thinks it is fun,
He cries when it's done.

Mike is my mate,
He really is great,
He says that he cares,
So I hug thin air.

Katie A Barnett (9)
South Park School, Fraserburgh

Mog

My dog Mog is like a fat hog,
and she looks like a log.
She's a poopin', loopin', pooper machine
Bog is her boyfriend I don't know why
but he's like a pie and is really shy
and that's the story of my dog Mog.

Kirsten J Taylor (9)
South Park School, Fraserburgh

Motorbikes

Some motorbikes are very fast,
Some go out with a blast,
The engine sounds very cool,
Whoever wants to ride one is a fool,
I know someone that is very cruel,
People that have motorbikes really like to show 'em,
That is the end of my motorbike poem

Stephen Lippe (9)
South Park School, Fraserburgh

Scotland

Scotland, Scotland is the best,
You're mair better an the rest.
You're better an England, Ireland and France,
Fan Scotland play fitbae we always hae a chance.

Mair-more, an-than, fan-when, fitbae-football, hae-have.

Andrew Pirie (9)
South Park School, Fraserburgh

Shopping Spring

Shop to shop from bottom to top,
Oh boy I love shopping
Sometimes my feet get sore
And once I even started hopping.

Sometimes I buy make-up,
Sometimes I buy food,
And when I get home,
I feel really good.

Laura Hepburn (9)
South Park School, Fraserburgh

My PlayStation 2 Game

My PlayStation 2 game is
Called 'The Simpsons Hit and Run'
I play it all the time
It's really good fun
I get The Simpsons characters in every level
When you crash into stuff you feel like a devil,
When I play it I'm never sad
I think it's the best game I've ever had.

Craig Barbour (9)
South Park School, Fraserburgh

School

School, school it's not very cool.
In the summertime we wish we had a pool,
We think if you're a teacher you're a fool
I wish that my friends and I could rule the school!

David Clark (9)
South Park School, Fraserburgh

Night

Stars are bright.
They come out during the night.
The moon comes out too.
So it can stare down at you.
But there are a few
That hate the night,
Not like me
I think it's a pretty sight.

Emma McRae (9)
South Park School, Fraserburgh

Brother

My brother, my brother
I wish I had another
He plays his guitar
And thinks he's a star
I jump up and down
And all around
To tell him to
Stop and guess
What he did . . .
He kicked me a lot . . .
Yip that's my brother.

Marc Noble (9)
South Park School, Fraserburgh

Frog

Jump, jump, jump away, jump up to the sky
Goodbye frog, goodbye.
Jump, jump, jump away, jump up to the stars
Then come back down and swing on the monkey bars.
Jump, jump, jump away, jump into the pond,
You know I am quite fond of you.

Lauren Buchan (9)
South Park School, Fraserburgh

My Sister

My sister has long hair,
She tells on me and it's not fair,
She hits me with lots of things,
I cover my ears when she sings.

Her friends always come over to play,
That is Danica and Cara I hate to say,
When they are over God help us all,
For they really have a ball.

She always shows off,
But when she's in trouble she
Always gets let off.

Andrew Reid (9)
South Park School, Fraserburgh

My Fish

I like fish
But not on a dish,
I have one myself
As small as a tiny toy elf,
She has a tank
And her mind is very blank
Starky is her name,
She was very shy when she came,
But now she's fine
And I'm telling you her belly sure does shine!
I like to stroke her but I get quite wet,
I'm glad she's not in the sea in case she gets caught in a net!

Erin Beaton (9)
South Park School, Fraserburgh

Lost!

'Ma! Ma! I canna find ma a book,'
'Weel Declan ga and hae a look.'
'Oh aricht Ma just a wee search.'
'Declan, I see it in the aul birch.'
'Ta, Ma, I really love you and that's nae a lee.'
'Aye, Declan, come and hae your tea.'

'Ye ken this, Ma, I canna find me fork!'
'Gang and hae a look before I eat your pork.'
'Look, Declan, there it is in the dra.'
'Cheers, Ma, oh did I say ta?'

'Ging and dee your homework,'
'Dae I have ta, Ma, it makes me a real dork?'
'Aye you do so do it quick.'
'Mam! Mam! Can I go outside? There's Dick.'
'Alricht just for a wee while,'
'Thanks, Ma, but I canna find ma shoes.'
'Here they are you are sometimes a richt coo.'

'Ma! Ma! I canna see ma jacket!'
'Shh! Be quiet you're always a right racket!
'Come inside it's time for beed.'
'But, Mam, I really dinna want my beed.'
'I'm nae caring, Dec, before you make me reed!'
'I really hate you, Mam, and that's nae a lee.'
'Aye, but fit would you do without me.'

Darren Milne (11)
Stuartfield Primary School, Peterhead

Stupid School

I am a football fan,
I also like toast and jam,
I am so fantastic,
All my friends act sarcastic,
I don't like to be alone,
I just wish I had a clone,
I know others who sit at the square,
And they like to sell ladies' underwear,
I also like a lot of hockey but,
Definitely not a stupid jockey,
I really like to play with my friends,
Playing tig and making dens,
I must admit I really hate school,
It is boring and makes me drool,
And when I see a scary teacher,
It makes me think of a tiny creature,
But I just think it is a shame,
That stupid old school has to be so *lame!*

Luke Duncan (11)
Stuartfield Primary School, Peterhead

Autumn Has Arrived

The autumn leaves swirl round and round,
They never ever touch the ground,
The wind grows stronger then dies down,
The colours are golden like a crown,
The last summer day has come to an end,
So what's the use for us to pretend?
We have no summer anymore,
Shouldn't we just close the door?
What's the point if we have to wait?
Summer won't have us back at this rate!

Stefanie Rhind (11)
Stuartfield Primary School, Peterhead

Animals

When you step outside and look to the skies
Or down to the ground
What do you find?
Birds, bees, ants, ladybirds and spiders,
The list could go on and on
Our world is filled with animals
If you need someone to talk to no one's there to hear
Or see you when you feel the world is against you
In some ways animals can be your best friends
They listen to all your opinions and never argue back
They're there for you through thick and thin
Good and bad
Happy and sad
Animals are people's best friends
And are there till the end
Never forget animals are a person's best friends.

Rachel McGinley (11)
Stuartfield Primary School, Peterhead

Outsider

As I look out of the window,
I see lots of things though all in shadow,
I'm the one who's always left out,
I'm the one they all talk about,
They don't realise I have feelings too,
Despite what they say I know that it's true,
I'm an outsider but who'd want to be
A person who picks on people like me?
So that's why everyone is so very sad,
I'm sorry but that's the impression I've had,
All of my life and probably after,
I'm sick and tired of hearing their laughter,
So if you are ever new to a place,
It's better to be an outsider with grace.

Emma-Lee Davidson (11)
Stuartfield Primary School, Peterhead

The View From The Portacabin Window

As I sit doing my work
I hear a sudden noise outside!
Looking up, I see a torturing sight,
A class going on the bus for a school trip!
Seeing this I forget my work and envy those children
Then I catch sight of the playground:
Green grass showing through
Why can't we sit on it?
Sure, it's wet, but it's our choice!
And do I see the Primary sixes?
It's a bit blurred but they're obviously having fun!
At this moment I decide life is officially unfair,
Hmm . . . it's quite sunny outside,
But judging by my luck, I've probably forgotten my sunglasses.
And it turns out, I also forgot to do my work.
Oh well!

Beth Ann Gordon (11)
Stuartfield Primary School, Peterhead

A Funny Monster

A funny monster to me is blue and incredibly fluffy,
He wears red boxers on his head.
He'd have little arms and little legs
And a body that you could use to bounce to the moon.
He'd wear a Superman costume and try to fly away.
He'd have hands soft enough to fall asleep in,
He'd watch cartoon on TV and play all sorts of games.

A funny monster to me would take you to a far away land.
He wouldn't have wings he'd have magic and different things.
He tries to make people laugh but he's really, really clumsy.
Inside he's a ball of fluff,
It wouldn't matter what you like he'd always like you.

That is my funny monster you may have a different one,
But I bet you want yours to come alive as well.

Jack Stott (11)
Stuartfield Primary School, Peterhead

I'm A Celebrity Get Me Out Of Here!

We're in the helicopter, we're in the air,
At the end of this I will have dirty hair.
We have reached the jungle and it looks hot,
I think I will have a good time (not!).
Ant and Dec are very funny,
And I hope it will not be too sunny.
We are all getting friendly but it is just the start,
And I hope my heart won't go mad,
Because I might get really sad,
I will try to be happy to get your vote,
And I really do hope
I will be queen of the jungle which is my dream,
To become a queen!
It's nearly the end and I am still here,
I hope I get lots and lots of beer.
There's just two of us now,
I hope I wasn't a cow!
Now it's the final and we are waiting,
When I get home I will start some baking,
Ant and Dec announce the winner,
Now I am ready for my dinner.
'And the winner is . . . '
Me, yes, yes I won
Now it's all over and done!

Jenna Elaine Thomson (11)
Stuartfield Primary School, Peterhead

Leave Me Alone!

Stop pinching and
Stop poking me
Go away,
Leave me alone!

Can't you see?
I've tried to get away
But I can't,
Leave me alone!

Yell no more
Don't whine
I've done nothing to you,
Leave me alone!

Finally! You've left me alone
But it's boring
I can't shout at anyone anymore,
Please come back!

Danielle Jade Harper (10)
Stuartfield Primary School, Peterhead

Best Friends

You and me are best friends
We'll stick together till the end
We'll ride our bikes and gang for hikes
We'll do anything you like
We do everything together
It doesn't matter about the weather
Whether it's hot
Or whether it's not.

We help in the town
Delivering things all around
We don't want pay
We'll just work away
Till the very next day.

We'll play in the yard
We'll draw on some card
We won't get bored
'Be quiet!' Mum will roar.

Whatever the weather
No matter the weather
We'll always be together
Forever!

Nicola Ann Munro (11)
Stuartfield Primary School, Peterhead

Where's My Chocolate?

My mammy gave me a penny.
I went straight to the shop.
I bought a chocolate that I liked,
And I put it in my pocket.
The very next day I tried to take it out,
But it pulled me in my pocket
And I couldn't get back out.

It took me to a creepy cave,
And I had a little lamp.
I saw a huge dragon,
He had ears as big as walls.
He had a chocolate in his hand,
I thought it could be mine,
Is it the one I just bought from Nickle 'n' Dime.

The dragon took a little taste
He didn't like it much,
He thought, *ouch well I'll throw it to the Dutch!*
I stole a jet went all the way,
And still I could not find,
That day that I remember,
Will be inside my mind.

Kieran Connolly (11)
Stuartfield Primary School, Peterhead

Nonsense Rhymes

There once was a donkey
Who had a monkey
There once was a man
Who had a lamb
There once was a brain
Who had a chain
There once was a boy
Who had a toy
There once was a fox
Who had a box
There once was a block
Who had a clock
There once was a grandma
There once was a tool
Who had a pool
There once was a girl
Who had a knitted purl
There once was a light
Who had a fight
There once was a bend
And that's the end!

Kobi Poole (11)
Stuartfield Primary School, Peterhead

Tia

Tia is a young German Shepherd
She lives with her family in Stuartfield.

One day her family took her out for a walk
Along one of the old railway lines.

She was running along the railway line
When she saw somebody in the distance.

Then she started running faster and faster
And the family was shouting
'Tia come back!'

There was no sign of her
But then they saw something coming towards them.

It was Tia but she was bleeding
Her family went running towards her.

They thought to themselves who might have done this to her,
Tia knew but she couldn't tell them
So they never found out.

Tanya Rose Rennie (11)
Stuartfield Primary School, Peterhead

Vulcanic

I am Vulcanic from Vulcan
I'm 130,000 years old
I may not look that strong on the outside
But on the inside I'm quite bold.

I come and go whenever I like
And collect tattoos from everywhere
And with my three connected eyes
There are many people I scare.

I have no hair on the top of my head
And I have fiery legs
I have fire and ice packs
And daggers on my hands not pegs.

I have 18 toes on my feet
And I like things that are like black
But whenever I leave Earth I always say
'I'll be back.'

Christopher Ian Kelman (10)
Westhill Primary School, Westhill

Bedbugs

My alien is the bedbug
He comes from the planet Mars
My alien is like a wiggly worm
With eyes like telescopes
My alien's neck is as long as a giraffe
And his body wobbles like a plate of jelly
His claws are as sharp as knives
And shine like silver
His teeth are red and pointed like a dagger
My alien's tail is like a rattlesnake
And his skin is a s tough as leather
He is as strong as an ox
So you'd better watch out for the bedbugs.

Lauren Gale (12)
Westhill Primary School, Westhill

Megorna

Megorna is as strong as ten oxen
He is as tall as a house
He has tentacles that suck things up like a Hoover
And he might have a big head
But his brain is the size of a pea.
He is blind as a bat
His legs are harder than steel.
He can smell as bad as a gone off milk.
He can camouflage himself like two zebras together
His sense of smell is as good as a dog's
And his claws are as sharp as a shark's tooth.
His attitude is as bad as a tree's.
He is as heavy as 1,655,247,829 tons.
Oh! And two thin men!
His stomach is as big as a lorry
And his feet make him walk on air like on the moon
He is as quiet as night, takes part instead of day
And he eats flying blue pigs with his tail.

Kern Lasoki (11)
Westhill Primary School, Westhill

The Reptilian

My skin is as blue as the deep blue sea.
I'm as nimble as a goat.
I can float like a cloud.
I can skim across water like a jetski.
I'm as strong as an ox.
My tail is as long as an elephant's trunk.
My red eyes are as bright as fire.
I have hearing like Daredevil.
I'm as clever as Professor Stephen Hawking.
My breath is as deadly as cyanide.
I can jump as far as a frog.
I'm as serious as a judge.

Jack Molyneux (12)
Westhill Primary School, Westhill

My Alien Chester

Chester's eyes are like Pluto floating in space
His stomach is like colourful shooting stars
His hair is like a spiked point in grooves.
Chester's head is like a ripe watermelon sitting on a plum
His mouth is like a black hole sucking in everything in its path
His ears are like little roses floating in the blue sky.
Chester's eyebrows are like worms looking for cover
His hands are like claws waving madly.
His legs are like spikes striking into the surface
Chester's cheeks are like miniature green fields
His nose is like a hawk's beak peering down on the plain
Chester, the alien, is like a force beyond belief.

Cory Ogden (11)
Westhill Primary School, Westhill

Froz

Froz's hair is a glittery green
It shines and sparkles like a disco ball
He has pink pompoms on golden rods
His eyes are swirly and blue
Like the Mediterranean Sea
His nose is a deep purple
Froz's teeth are blue and silver
And sparkle like no other
He has a purple body with orange spots
Looks like Froz got the chickenpox
His legs are wriggly and spotty as well
His arms are like sticks off trees.

Alyssa Warren (11)
Westhill Primary School, Westhill

Octerpent

I have an eye like a hawk
I have tentacles like an octopus
I have two fangs like a snake
I also have a tongue like a snake
I have hearing like a fox
I have hair as grey as an old granny
I have lips like a girl
I have come from somewhere as remote as Pluto
My ears are like antennae
My scales are as yellow as the sun
My body is as green as grass and
My eyes are as black as coal.

Kieran Walden (11)
Westhill Primary School, Westhill

George

His hair is like a hedgehog
With spikes as sharp as needles
His eyes are like lasers
Red-hot and flashing
His ears are like elephants'
Large and wrinkly too
He has as many arms as an octopus
With suckers on them too
His legs are as straight as tree trunks
And teeth as sharp as sharks
With a grin from ear to ear
He's a very friendly alien.

Calum Walker (11)
Westhill Primary School, Westhill

Steve-Becca

Steve-Becca is a two-headed monster with some great abilities,
His/her name comes from the names Steven and Rebecca.
Steve-Becca can fly as fast as a golden eagle.
Steve-Becca can run as fast as a cheetah.
Their wing-span can reach as long as 1 metre.
Steve-Becca is 75cm tall.
Steve-Becca's body is as scaly as a chameleon.
Their wings are as delicate as a butterfly.
Their pointed arms are as sharp as sharks' teeth.
Steve's hair is as brown as fresh bark.
Becca's teeth are as clean as diamonds (they *are* diamonds!)
Their blue spots are as blue as the sea.

Craig Cuthbertson (11)
Westhill Primary School, Westhill

The Lady Of Love

I am the lady of love
I am as big as your heart
I am as gentle as a dove
I am as calm as the sea
I am as colourful as a rainbow
And as pretty as can be.

My hair is like a picture on a Valentine's Day card
My eyes are like diamonds glistening in the moonlight
My smile is as bright as a star in the sky
As you can see I am full of love and care and share
And as lovely as can be
And that's the end of a poem about me.

Lauren Swinhoe (11)
Westhill Primary School, Westhill

Monty

My name is Monty
I come from Zephyr
My hair is like pink fur
My three eyes are like ping-pong balls
My three legs are like a giraffe so tall
My nose is like an upside down pear
My tongue is like a snake's, so beware
My ears are like an elephant's skin
My fingers are like bones, long and thin
My nails are like a sky that's black
My teeth are like shiny glass
But if I look in a mirror, it might just crack!

Ross Taylor (11)
Westhill Primary School, Westhill

Shnarp

My eyes are like a sniper's spotting my next target,
My ears are like radar dishes moving round and hearing everything,
My claws are as sharp as dinosaurs,
My teeth are like steak knives cutting and breaking any meat.
My body is as hard as titanium,
The Earth is doomed as a fly,
My legs are like a stable tripod.
My arms are as fast as a bullet.
I am as powerful as an angry bull.

Andrew James Skinner (11)
Westhill Primary School, Westhill

Fang

Fang's eyes are like a swirling vortex,
He has a nose as long as a carrot.
Fang has teeth as long as a mile,
His body as bright as the sun.
Fang has arms as red as Mars,
He has legs as straight as rulers.
Fang has an ear like a violin,
The other had flames like a fire.
Fang has hair as blue as the sea,
His shoulders were jagged like rocks.
Fang has feet that stick to the ground like glue,
Fang has three fingers as wriggly as worms,
Fang is a strange creature just like me.

Kerry Milne (11)
Westhill Primary School, Westhill

Spike

His arms and legs are as long as a slithering snake
His tail as sharp as a spear
His mouth is like a blob
The fire from his tummy is like the fire from a dragon
His body is like a very big boulder
His mouth like a mini half moon
His many eyes have laser beams that light up the night sky
Two hands and two of his feet are like half of a flower
His one strand of hair is like the hair of a baby
His fifth arm is like a sharp knife
His ears are as big as elephants' ears
His crown is like a king's crown sparking in the sun.

Fiona Dixon (11)
Westhill Primary School, Westhill

Puff

My face is as round as a ball
My eyes are large and bright with my curls that swing out at the side
My nose is as sharp as a knife and my teeth are long and white.
With a body of tin and a smile that will grin
You'll definitely see me at night!

I have six octopus arms that can cling nice and tight,
So you'd better watch out, as you might get a fright!

I have a funny hat and an earring in one ear
But if someone touches me, I get a scare and I will then disappear.
That is when they scream and shout and after that I will never
come out.

Stephanie McMillan (11)
Westhill Primary School, Westhill

Trixy

Trixy is an alien
She is wonderful
She is bright
Her hair can be
As messy as a mop
Her clothes are as
Creased as a granny's face.

Trixy is a beautiful loving alien
She has a boyfriend his name is John
John is tall, chubby and sweet
Trixy is small, thin and very nice and sweet.

Jacqueline Wilson (11)
Westhill Primary School, Westhill

Rocky

My name is Rocky, I have long green hair like snake skin.
My golden teeth shine as bright as stars.
I have long arms, as strong as stone.
My fingers are as rough as rock.
My legs stretch out all around and help me run fast like a spider.
On the end of my feet my toenails are sharp as razors.
My eyes can see everything, they bob about like springs.
I have long eyelashes like spaghetti.
The skin on my face is wrinkled and shiny like leather.
I have a long, thin, forked tongue just like a snake's.
In the middle of my body it's a huge grey rock
It's covered in moss which is soft like a teddy's fur.
My eyebrows are big and busy like caterpillars'.

Calum Watson (11)
Westhill Primary School, Westhill

Pinky

My alien Pinky comes from Mars
She really is quite bizarre!
Her ears are as yellow as a lemon
Her nose is like a Valentine love heart
Her teeth are as purples as a snail's shell
The stars on her tummy are sparkling like glitter
She is as colourful as a rainbow
Her legs are like an octopus
Her legs are spotty like a Dalmatian
Her right arm is as green as apples
Her feet are like horses' hooves
Pinky is going back to Mars to visit her family
But she will be back for a visit next week.

Naomi Howitt (11)
Westhill Primary School, Westhill

Apocolips

His eyes are as cold as a winter morning.
His mouth is as cruel as the storm.
He flies like a hawk snoopily around.
His body is like a wound spring waiting to pounce.
His hands are like spiders waiting to move.
Sometimes he feels as sad as an outcast sitting in his cave alone.
He can run faster than a cheetah, pelting at full speed.
His legs are chunkier than trees.
His mood changes quicker than traffic lights.
But his heart is slowly growing like a flower in the morning.
His eyes are slowly getting warmer and softer.
He is changing into a hero . . .
Because he has a friend!

Fraser W McKain (12)
Westhill Primary School, Westhill

Zorrog

I am Zorrog
I'm related to the morning
My eyes are as red as lava
My hair is as green as grass
My body is as spotty as a Dalmatian
My arms are as long as a python
My nails are as sharp as knives
I am as a ugly as a pig
And as quick as a cat
I am as sneaky as a monkey
I'm related to the marrog
Zarrog.

David Alexander Wright (11)
Westhill Primary School, Westhill

Polly From Pluto

She's pink and fluffy like fresh candyfloss
She's as big as the moon
She is Polly from Pluto
As fit as a baboon.

Her tummy is as spotty as a big round Easter egg
Her eyes are as bright as the sun
Her nose is as pointy as an eagle's beak
She is as quiet as a nun.

She's magic like a fairy
She hovers like a helicopter
Her 3 big toes are as furry as a monkey
She is as healthy as a doctor.

She's pink and fluffy like fresh candyfloss
She's as big as the moon
She is Polly from Pluto
As fit as a baboon.

Natalie Watt (12)
Westhill Primary School, Westhill

Space

Meteors whizz through space
Like racing express trains.
Twinkling stars glitter
As bright as light bulbs in the sky.
Speeding comets fly past
Their tails gleaming like silver ribbons.
Black holes suck up planets
Like a vampire in the night.
An alien space ship glides through space
As quiet as a whisper.

Mark Drummond (11)
Westhill Primary School, Westhill

Rocky

Rocky the doggy demon is a menace
He has claws like steel
And has wing tips of gold
At his feet all his enemies kneel.

He's got shiny armour that could withstand diamonds
With a helmet that could hold off the heaviest blows
And has teeth like daggers
Into his lair no one goes.

He has the strength of an ox
And the agility of a cheetah
With his senses he can see as far as an owl
And hears better than a bat
And with that this poem is concluded by Peter.

Peter Ronald (11)
Westhill Primary School, Westhill

Deep In Outer Space

Banana yellow, crescent moon
Like a huge smile, later a full moon.

Dazzling, shining, shooting star
Travels as fast as a Ferrari car.

Hazy, misty, swirling gases
Like a whirlwind with rock masses.

Red-hot burning sun
Is as heavy as a tonne.

Bulky, rocky, hurtling asteroid
Like a falling rock in an empty void.

Ruaridh Gollifer (11)
Westhill Primary School, Westhill